Harvest

Also available in this series
_____

Forthcoming in this series
_____

Harvest

Sam Inglis

continuum
NEW YORK • LONDON

2004

The Continuum International Publishing Group Inc
15 E 26 Street, New York, NY 10010

The Continuum International Publishing Group Ltd
The Tower Building, 11 York Road, London SE1 7NX

www.continuumbooks.com

Printed in the United States of America

Library of Congress Cataloging-in-Publication Data
Inglis, Sam.
Harvest / Sam Inglis.
p. cm. — (33 1/3)
/ISBN 0-8264-1495-8 (pbk. : alk. paper)
1. Young, Neil. Harvest moon. I. Title. II. Series.
ML420.Y75I54 2003

782.42166'092—dc21ISBN 0-8264-1495-8

Contents

Harvest

"Young's search for shelter from the storm resonates like a heartbeat," concluded *Rolling Stone*'s four-star review. Its author, Greg Kot, traced the songs along "a path from restlessness to reaffirmation," describing "a hushed musical landscape at times populated only by a ghostly harmonica, a few spooky bass lines and Young's cracked, lonesome tenor."

The year was 1992; the album, *Harvest Moon* by Neil Young. Twenty years after the release of his best-selling LP, Young had at last done what his fans had stopped expecting him to do. He'd reformed the band that had backed him on *Harvest*, picked up his acoustic guitar and recorded a follow-up. The resulting album was almost a remake of its predecessor. Just as on *Harvest*, Young fleshed out a core of country-tinged ballads with a solo live recording, and hired his old friend Jack Nitzsche to provide an orchestral arrangement. He even called up the same celebrity backing singers who'd turned out all those years ago to add the finishing touches to his only major hit single, 'Heart Of Gold'.

Had *Harvest Moon* been released in 1973, Young would have been accused of standing still, of degenerating into self-pastiche. In 1992, however, it was greeted as the end of a great musical journey. In the two decades that separated *Harvest* from its sequel, Neil Young had gone from hippy hero to reactionary redneck and back. Shocked and appalled by the stardom *Harvest* had brought him, he'd abandoned its winsome, country-tinged style and struck out for unknown shores. In a quest to lose his newfound audience, he'd produced everything from ear-bleeding rock music to experimental electronica. In the 80s, Young had gone so far "out there" that few thought he'd make it back; but back he was, and *Harvest Moon* was final confirmation of one of the most remarkable resurgences in rock history. Not so much a return to form as a trip back in time, it showed Young accepting at last what everyone else knew: that the original *Harvest* was a classic album, and should be celebrated as such.

It's a nice story, but the truth is more complicated. In 1992, Neil Young was back in the fold, lauded as the only artist of his generation still making essential music. It seemed obvious then that his most popular record must be an essential album, but it hadn't always looked that way. *Rolling Stone* itself had panned *Harvest* on release, John Mendelssohn's scathing review salted with phrases like "half-assed baloney", "flatulent and portentous nonsense" and "weariest clichés". Throughout the 70s, a succession of rock writers portrayed *Harvest* as an album of superficial beauty, barren of new ideas or real emotion. Stephen Holden summed up the view of many when he described it as Young's "most compromised album".

Not all critics were as negative as *Rolling Stone*'s: the British music press, for instance, accorded rave reviews to both *Harvest* and 'Heart Of Gold'. Yet it would be fair to say that *Harvest* was a hit despite the press, rather than because of them; and it's not only rock critics who have expressed distaste for Young's most successful album. Ask serious Neil Young fans to name their favourite album of his and you'll hear votes for any one of ten or so, but *Harvest* is unlikely to be among them. If you love Young for the searing rock 'n' roll of *Rust Never Sleeps* or the raw emotion of *Tonight's The Night*, *Harvest* is too safe, too bland, too popular.

In the few interviews he's given since its release, Neil Young has played along with the idea that *Harvest* was an aberration, and that its success drove him to seek the musical wilderness. When he compiled his triple-album retrospective *Decade*, he included half of *Harvest*, but undermined 'Heart Of Gold' with an equivocal liner note: "This song put me in the middle of the road. Travelling there soon became a bore so I headed for the ditch. A rougher ride but I met more interesting people there." When he did eventually record the sequel, he gave the impression of having suffered twenty years' sustained pressure to do so: "When people start asking you to do the same thing again and again," he told *Rolling Stone*'s Alan Light, "that's when you know you're way too close to something that you don't want to be near."

It may well be true that Young had been taken aback by *Harvest*'s popularity, and there's no doubt that it made him afraid of being pigeonholed as a tasteful, country-tinged singer-songwriter. "I just didn't want to do the obvious thing, because it didn't feel right," he said to Light. Nevertheless, there's also an element of self-mythologising in comments like these. From the reception accorded to *Harvest Moon*, you might think he'd spent the decades that separated the two albums trying to eliminate all trace of *Harvest*'s sound from his music. If so, you'd be surprised by albums like 1978's *Comes A Time*, which is every bit as tuneful and polished as his biggest hit. You'd also have to wonder why Young has returned so regularly to the same musicians, the same studio and the same producer.

The truth is that although Young refused to deliver a second *Harvest* immediately, he was ready to return to it long before the rest of the world was. *Harvest* caught the crest of a wave, when Young's profile was already at its highest and mellow singer-songwriters were flavour of the month. *Harvest Moon* would also appear at a high-water mark in Young's career, when its gentleness would form a timely acknowledgement that grunge's moment had passed. *Comes A Time*, by contrast, was released when punk rock was at its height, and although it was a better album than *Harvest* or *Harvest Moon*, it could not achieve the same career-defining status. The next time Young went back to Nashville, in 1982, he recorded an album he described as being "like *Harvest* II". His record company wouldn't even let him release it: being a tasteful, country-tinged singer-songwriter was *so* ten years ago.

Thanks to the success of 1989's *Freedom*, Young was eventually able to create a climate in which the *Harvest* sound could thrive once again. The critics fell for *Harvest Moon* and forgot the disdain they'd held for the original. *Harvest* had, at last, been admitted into the canon of Classic Albums.

Neil Young's own attitude to *Harvest* has been more consistent, but more complex. He's proud of it, thinks it was a good record, but doesn't want to be defined by *Harvest* alone. It was just "a mellow trip, where my life was at the time; but only for a couple of months." Shortly after the sequel was released, Young summed up what the original meant to him in a typically qualified way. "It was probably the finest record I ever made," he said, "but that's really a restricting adjective for me."

This is the most insightful analysis Neil Young has ever offered of his own work. Finesse, it suggests, can be impressive and difficult to achieve, but it is not enough to make something into a work of art. It's something we associate with craft, with small detail, with skill in the employment of tools. We might describe a perfectly executed architectural drawing or a hand-built replica of the Cutty Sark as "fine", but not a Rothko painting or a Dostoevsky novel. Finesse and refinement are admirable qualities, but they are not the artist's ultimate goals; and, indeed, they can stand in the way of those goals.

The genius of albums like *Tonight's The Night* or *Everybody Knows This Is Nowhere* lies in Young's rejection of craft for its own sake. Instrumental proficiency is treated with disdain, while the studio is used simply as a means of capturing a moment, raw and unadulterated. Young's guitar playing is remarkable not for any delicate nuances but for its brutal effectiveness, as in the definitive one-note solo on 'Cinnamon Girl'. His best songs are great not because they place chords together in clever and interesting ways, but because they bypass the intellect and go straight for the heartstrings. His most memorable performances are not his most controlled and pitch-perfect, but those that bring a searing emotional intensity to the song.

These qualities are not brought to the fore on *Harvest* in the same way as they are on other Neil Young albums. Its delicate tunes provide an exhibition of classic songwriting technique, but they don't seem to shine a bare light bulb onto the soul as some Young songs do. The musical backing never lapses into tweeness, but nor does it give voice to howls of pain or torrents of rage. By Neil Young's standards *Harvest* is a pleasant rather than a passionate album, one which comes more from the head than the heart. Yet, as his subsequent career demonstrates, Neil Young's standards are not shared by everyone.

Some artists become defined among fans and casual listeners alike by their most popular work. Every subsequent Al Stewart album is seen as a better or worse approximation to the template established by *Year Of The Cat*; Steely Dan produced their own archetype in *Aja*. In other cases, though, serious followers and dabblers come to opposing views. The success of 'Walk On The Wild Side' and *Transformer* planted Lou Reed in the public eye as a leather-clad cartoon figure, but the cognoscenti prefer the darker pleasures of *Berlin* and *Street Hassle*. To the world at large, Neil Young was defined by *Harvest*, a melancholic songwriter bursting with catchy tunes, smiling awkwardly with a prairie straw in his mouth. To those who feel they know his music well, by contrast, the real Neil Young is defined almost in opposition to the one presented on his most popular album. Many fans and critics dismiss the singer of 'Heart Of Gold' in favour of the equally romanticised Young they hear on *Tonight's The Night*, brought so low by despair and drink that he is almost unable to sing.

This is unfair both to *Harvest* and to the millions of people who've bought it over the years. The genius of Young's despatches from the ditch does not render *Harvest*'s more subtle virtues worthless, nor make it any less compelling to listen to in its own right. *Harvest* is no *Lou Reed Live*, cobbled together by showy musicians and a cynical record company with virtually no input from the man himself. Neil Young hands over the reins to no-one, and *Harvest* is as much his sole creation as *Tonight's The Night* or *Rust Never Sleeps*. It's less confessional, less nakedly emotive than those albums, but it's not impersonal. It's gentler and lighter, but it is far from bland. It presents Young's individuality in a more accessible manner, but never effaces that individuality. And even those fans who consider *Harvest* a sell-out cannot wish that it had never been made; for if Neil Young hadn't found the middle of the road, he would never have ended up in the ditch.

A Journey Through The Past

Neil Young is one of those artists who always sounds like himself. Throughout his long career he's dabbled in almost every genre of popular music: folk music, rock music, country music, pop music, blues music. His changes of style have brought varying degrees of success, but even his pastiches of other artists are instantly recognisable as Neil Young records. Some of his work is highly personal, but all of it is extremely individual.

Although Young was only 26 when he recorded *Harvest*, he was already a veteran in the pop business. Music had been an all-consuming interest since his childhood, when he'd been something of a misfit at school in Canada. Polio had left his body weak down the left-hand side, a weakness about which he was acutely self-conscious. His parents Scott and Rassy divorced when he was 12; Scott remained in Toronto with Neil's elder brother Bob, while Neil went with Rassy to make a new start in Winnipeg. He would spend his nights listening to American pop stations on the radio, and his evenings practising the guitar with school bands.

His first real band, The Squires, initially played mainly Shadows-style guitar instrumentals. They achieved some popularity in Canada, but Young's ambitions stretched further afield, musically and geographically. Even then, he wasn't willing to accept that a musician might have to be restricted to one style. Although he was painfully sensitive about his singing voice, he desperately wanted to be a singer. He heard The Rolling Stones and wanted the same freedom to rock out; he heard Bob Dylan and wanted to write songs that went beyond throwaway pop. He wanted to play in coffee houses and bars as well as school halls.

The Squires diversified musically, introducing more of Young's own songs — not to mention his increasingly psychotic guitar solos — and touring further around Canada, but major success eluded them and they eventually disintegrated. Young's parallel career as a coffee-house singer-songwriter also failed to blossom, while his last shot at success in Canada saw him join a characteristically genre-bending band. The Mynah Birds combined black soul and white rock music and briefly flew high, signing and recording for Motown. They were then shot down before they could even release a record, when it turned out that singer Rick James was missing without leave from the US Navy.

When The Mynah Birds collapsed, Neil Young decided not to waste any more time trying to make it big in Canada. In 1966, Los Angeles was the place to be, a court of fashionable counter-culture built around groups like The Byrds and The Mamas and The Papas. These bands were proving what Young had always felt, that musicians didn't have to stick to one style of music. The Byrds crunched together Dylanesque folk and Beatlesque pop with a healthy dose of experimentation on top, and the results were always on the radio. This, surely, was the place and time when Young's eclecticism could work to his advantage.

Neil Young entered America illegally with five fellow Canadians, including bass player Bruce Palmer. Driving an ageing hearse, they duly made their way to the City of Angels in search of stardom; and perversely, it was Young's Canadian connections that would come good in LA, when his hearse was spotted on the freeway by Stephen Stills. An American singer Young had befriended back in Fort William, Stills had also come to LA to make his fortune, dragging in his wake fellow singer-songwriter Richie Furay. Stills, Young, Furay and Palmer formed a group, roping in another Canadian, drummer Dewey Martin. The Buffalo Springfield took their name from a company that made mowers and their sound from any number of different sources. This would be the band that could foster both Young's serious folkie side and his wild guitar solos, a band that could record two-chord pop songs or ambitious progressive pieces.

The Buffalo Springfield became major contenders in LA's alternative scene. Sharing bills with the likes of Love and The Doors, they acquired a reputation as an excellent live act, and great things were expected of them on signing to Atlantic Records. Expectations were, for the most part, unfulfilled. Despite the hype, their first album suffered from lacklustre production and poor sales. A throwaway Stephen Stills song, 'For What It's Worth', finally provided them with the hit they needed, but by this time, tensions between the band members, drugs, and the weight of expectation were beginning to tell.

Where Stephen Stills had a conventionally strong rock singer's voice, Young was desperately insecure about his own high-pitched, thin tone. At the same time, he very much wanted to sing his own songs, and was seldom happy when the other band members took lead vocal on them. As the band's troubles mounted Young began to suffer epileptic fits, while Palmer was jailed for cannabis possession and deported to Canada. By the time their second album *Buffalo Springfield Again* was released, the band was falling apart. Young left and rejoined several times before finally quitting to start a solo career.

It was during his time with Buffalo Springfield that Neil Young met composer Jack Nitzsche. They became close friends and embarked on an ambitious collaboration called 'Expecting To Fly', which took a month to record and was included on the second Springfield album, although Young was the only band member involved. It laid the foundation for Neil Young's first, self-titled solo album, an exhibition of clever arrangement and studio trickery, with layers of multitracked instrumentation often swamping Young's fragile voice. The exception was the closing track, 'The Last Trip To Tulsa', a surreal nine-minute solo acoustic song which saw Young revive the coffee-house folk strand of his musical personality.

A lot of hard work went into *Neil Young*, and the album was not a hit. Perhaps it was this that began to turn Young against elaborate production techniques; at any rate, he fell to jamming with an obscure Californian garage-rock band called The Rockets, and found the experience so refreshing that he appropriated them as his new backing band. In Buffalo Springfield, Young had often found himself the loser in band arguments; on his first solo album, his individuality had become overshadowed by dense arrangements and production.

Despite Nitzsche's encouragement, moreover, his singing had still sounded timid, as though he was overawed by the studio trickery and session talent on display.

Crazy Horse, as The Rockets were re-christened, eliminated both problems. There was no doubt that Young was the leader and they were his backing band. This time, he was the seasoned professional and they were the novices. At the same time, their presence provided a solid platform on which Young could build. It's hard to imagine Stephen Stills doing nothing but play the same two chords over and over again for ten minutes while Young launches into some epic guitar solo, but this was Crazy Horse's role from the beginning. They were and have always been the most basic of rock bands.

Young recorded one album with the original line-up of Crazy Horse. *Everybody Knows This Is Nowhere* was his second solo album, and a world away from his work with Jack Nitzsche. All artifice was cleared away. The songs were brutally simple three-chord affairs, the arrangements sparse, the performances for the most part live and undoctored. Young's confidence in his singing had clearly grown, although he still replaced his live vocals after the event.

Everybody Knows This Is Nowhere remains a favourite of both Young and his fans, but it was only a modest success at the time. Live shows both with Crazy Horse and without, in solo folkie mode, were well received, but Young's career as a solo artist would ultimately be established by joining yet another band.

While Young had been locked in the studio with Jack Nitzsche or deafening audiences in small clubs with Crazy Horse, his fellow Buffalo Springfield alumni had not been idle. The most successful by far was Stephen Stills. The turn of the 70s was the time of the super-group, when members of big-selling bands discarded their sidemen to indulge in self-important collabora-tions with one another. All too often, the sum of the illustrious parts would turn out to be vanishingly small, egos would clash, and the supergroupers would hastily begin solo careers. Crosby, Stills and Nash, however, hit the jackpot.

David Crosby was a pivotal figure in the LA scene, having become too alternative even for The Byrds. Nash had likewise become too involved in the counter-culture to continue playing with straight-laced English pop stars The Hollies. Neither they nor Stills had the option of returning to their established bands should their new group fail; and it did not. The imaginatively named Crosby, Stills and Nash recorded an album of ambitious, harmony-drenched hippy music. Salted with studio cleverness, it reached the US Top Ten and stayed in the charts for two years.

Stephen Stills had thus achieved infinitely greater post-Springfield success than Neil Young. He was at the core of perhaps the biggest new group in America, while Young was still playing small clubs and coffee-houses. Like Young, however, Stills didn't want to commit himself forever to one side of the acoustic/electric divide. Buffalo Springfield had combined folk and rock aesthetics to great effect, and Stills wanted his new group to do the same. To bolster CSN's rock power, it was agreed that an additional musician was required; and despite the arguments that had destroyed the Springfield, Stills felt that Young was the man for the job.

Neil Young's relationship with Stephen Stills was no easier within the cumbersomely named Crosby, Stills, Nash and Young than it had been in the days of Buffalo Springfield. Young's distaste for the painstaking, track-by-track recording techniques he'd used on his own first album was cemented by the sessions for CSNY's debut. Such was Stills' perfectionism that he later claimed it took eight hundred hours of studio time to record. Only three of the songs on *Déjà Vu* were true band performances by the entire group: on one of these, 'Woodstock', Young watched Stephen Stills erase his original live vocal to replace it with a more precise, but less magical retake. " 'Woodstock' was a great record at first," he later told Cameron Crowe. "Then, later on, they were in the studio for a long time and started nitpicking. . . . They did a lot of things over again that I thought were more raw and vital sounding."

Simply by joining CSNY, Neil Young had been propelled from obscurity to stardom. The American music business had spent years searching for a homegrown band that could rival the universal appeal of The Beatles, and CSNY seemed to be the most promising candidates since The Beach Boys. The release of *Déjà Vu* confirmed their status: it was the most eagerly anticipated album in years, selling over two million copies on advance orders alone. CSNY's live shows were huge, three-hour spectaculars, including in a prime slot at the Woodstock festival in August 1969. Yet Young's ambivalence over *Déjà Vu* was matched by some listeners and critics, who felt it smug and overblown. The negative aspects of musical superstardom were rapidly becoming apparent. Unwelcome, uncomprehending attention from fans and press; heavy drug use and rampant egos; arguments about money: all combined to sour the experience.

Like Stephen Stills, Neil Young still wanted to keep alive all the musical strands he'd developed. In CSNY, Stills tried to create a single band that could move between angelic harmony and fiery rock, delicate folk and dirty blues. Young, too, used CSNY as a vehicle for different sides of his musical personality: he could be left alone on stage with his acoustic guitar, call upon three powerful voices to add harmonies, or indulge in snarling guitar duels with Stills. Even so, Young's commitment to CSNY was only ever a part-time one, and he devoted equal energy to pursuing the different threads he'd begun in his solo career.

Foremost among these, at the time, was playing with Crazy Horse. Adding a touch of rock 'n' roll to a CSN gig was all very well, but the raw minimalism of his own band was something else entirely: a musical vision that was purely Neil Young's, and a forcefulness that was not constrained by folk niceties. Young interspersed CSNY rehearsals with Crazy Horse recording sessions, cutting almost enough material for a complete album. Then disaster struck. By the time Young returned from working on *Déjà Vu* to pick up the loose ends, Crazy Horse guitarist Danny Whitten had become a junkie, passing out on stage and failing to remember songs. Horrified, Young sacked the band and shelved most of what they'd recorded.

Young's first two solo albums had explored separate, very different threads of his musical vision. His third, *After The Goldrush*, brought a number of these threads together. The folk-club Neil Young, full of bizarre lyrical imagery and fancy acoustic guitar patterns, shone on mystical hippy numbers like 'Tell Me Why'. 'I Believe In You' and minor hit 'Only Love Can Break Your Heart' were the work of a sophisticated AOR balladeer, setting heart-to-heart verse to catchy melodies, while Neil Young the frenzied rocker made an appearance on 'Southern Man' and 'When You Dance I Can Really

Love'. Yet another of Young's multiple personalities was evident on his anguished cover of Don Gibson's 'Oh Lonesome Me'. This Young, previously glimpsed only on the title track of *Everybody Knows This Is Nowhere* and the instrumental that opened his first solo album, wore fringed jackets and cowboy boots. All of these characters would eventually populate *Harvest*, but Country Neil would become a lot more prominent.

Although *After The Goldrush* was musically diverse, it was the fullest and most coherent realisation yet of Young's very individual philosophy of recording. Rather than hire a professional studio, Young and producer David Briggs converted the basement of his house in Topanga Canyon, California into a recording space. Crazy Horse drummer Ralph Molina and CSNY bassist Greg Reeves set up their equipment in the cramped confines, where they were joined by a Neil Young fan who'd got very lucky indeed. Nils Lofgren was a talented guitarist who'd crashed Young's dressing room at a show the previous year: now he was in Young's house, recording his new album. The only fly in the ointment was Young's insistence that he play piano instead of his own instrument.

This was very much of a piece with Young's developing approach to recording, in which the driving urges were freshness and simplicity. He wanted musicians who could target the core of the song without obscuring it through spurious instrumental virtuosity; and he wanted an environment where they could relax and cut loose when they played it. There were overdubs on *After The Goldrush*, but the 'Woodstock' experience ensured that Young cut as much as possible live, including all his vocals.

After The Goldrush was a big hit, and has remained one of Young's best-loved albums. Not all critics were kind at the time, however, and some fans felt it sounded middle-of-the-road after the blast of fresh air that was *Everybody Knows This Is Nowhere*. Meanwhile, the price of stardom was continuing to escalate. CSNY fell to bitter arguing, while Young's marriage to Susan Acevedo collapsed. Desperate for peace and quiet, he sold his Topanga Canyon home and moved to a ranch in the hills near San Francisco. His back, weakened down the left-hand side by his childhood polio, gave way completely when he attempted to move a heavy slab of wood. The next year would revolve around hospital visits, powerful medication and enforced rest.

Young was, at least, not single for long. His romance with actress Carrie Snodgress blossomed while he was in hospital, and in 1971 she came to live with him on the ranch, bringing with her a bizarre entourage of friends, family and hangers-on. One of these, Carrie's mother Carolyn, would be the partial inspiration for *Harvest*'s title track. Carrie herself was clearly in Young's mind when he wrote another new song, 'A Man Needs A Maid'. With a heap of new experiences to digest and plenty of time to sit and write, this was a productive period in Neil Young's songwriting career.

Most of the songs on *Harvest*, plus a string of others which would show up on future albums, were written after Neil Young moved to the ranch in August 1970. At this stage, though, it seems that Young was planning to follow up *After The Goldrush* with something very unlike what would eventually appear. With Danny Whitten and thus Crazy Horse still incapable, Young was touring as a solo artist: and though he was ostensibly promoting *After The Goldrush*, he was eager to showcase some of his new material. Several of these shows, including one at UCLA's Royce Hall and two nights at Massey Hall in Toronto, were recorded, and Reprise announced the forthcoming release of a double live album. This would feature half a dozen new songs as well as highlights from Young's back catalogue, most notably two songs of his that had originally been recorded by Buffalo Springfield with Richie Furay singing lead.

The projected double album of live, solo acoustic performances might well have proved a success, especially given the enthusiasm that the shows themselves had generated. Plans for the album reached an advanced stage, to the point were the track listing was released to the press, but it never appeared. The reasons for this decision have never been entirely clear, but it doubtless had much to do with the imminent release of another live double album on which Young featured: CSNY's *Four Way Street*. Conflict within CSNY had reduced their productivity in the studio from limited to non-existent, yet public and record company were clamouring for a follow-up to the best-selling *Déjà Vu*. Given that CSNY boasted an excellent reputation as a live act, *Four Way Street* was the obvious solution.

Four Way Street was divided into an electric and an acoustic album. Although the latter boasted only three Young songs, its release in early 1971 was probably enough to render Young's own acoustic live album re-dundant, in a commercial if not an artistic sense. It's also possible that Young simply got cold feet about his own project. It is, after all, hard to imagine a more exposed format than an acoustic double live album, especially for an artist who was still nursing insecurity about his singing. Although he's continued to perform in solo acoustic mode throughout his career, Young has never committed more than one side of an album to documenting these performances.

Such was Young's eclecticism, moreover, that no single strand of his musical personality could dominate for long, and it was around this time that he began to pursue a totally new direction. He might have turned against the painstaking production techniques he and

Jack Nitzsche had employed on his first solo album, but he did not want to abandon his creative partnership with Nitzsche. The composer's role on *After The Goldrush* had been limited to some wild piano playing, but he and Young now had a more ambitious collaboration in mind. Nitzsche took 'A Man Needs A Maid' and another piano-based ballad, 'There's A World', and penned extravagant orchestral arrangements. Was this to be the template for Young's new album?

The follow-up to *After The Goldrush* could have ended up showcasing Folkie Neil, or it could have represented the first outing for Epic Neil. As it turned out, both styles would eventually feature, but neither would be the main event. Perhaps Neil Young had originally intended the orchestral style to dominate the new album; but by the time he got to record with the London Symphony Orchestra, he already had a future No. 1 in the bag from another source. The same willingness to experiment that brought Young to London also brought him to a recording studio in Nashville, and it was these sessions that would define the *Harvest* sound.

Ready For The Country

In 1971, as it is now, the music industry was based around four cities: New York, Los Angeles, London and Nashville. In England, or on the West or East Coast, you could find diversity. There were top-selling pop bands, but there were also world-class orchestras, jazz groups and thriving underground rock communities. Nashville, by contrast, was built almost entirely upon one kind of music: country music.

The entire country music industry seemed to exist in a parallel universe. It had its own record labels, run from Nashville and kept under tight control by a few all-powerful owners and managers. It had its own chart system, where stars could be No. 1 for weeks without registering at all on the pop charts; and it had its own channels for promoting music, through country radio stations and TV shows.

In the late 60s and early 70s, the country music business retained many traditions that had vanished from pop and rock music. The goal in rock music was no longer hit singles, at least for their own sake: it was successful albums. Rock artists, unlike many country stars, were free to choose their own material, and to record only their own songs. They were, moreover, becoming increasingly ambitious. The Beatles had demonstrated that pop and rock recordings need not simply be the literal record of a band's live performance, but could be confected through imaginative use of technology. This, naturally, was a difficult process, requiring months in the studio. The shift to albums as the primary format for selling music allowed bands to extend the idea of the pop song, from complex multi-part pieces with pseudo-classical overtones to lengthy jams. A pop band like The Buffalo Springfield was more than just an assemblage of competent musicians thrown together to back a singer: it was a group of people working together as one unit, realising a collective musical vision.

Country music in 1971 had taken on few of these new ideas. For the most part, record company bosses, producers and A & R men had effective control over what songs their artists recorded and how they should sound. Some artists had their own back-up bands, but most of the playing on country records was done by professional session musicians — and it was done quickly. The specialty of Nashville was the mass production of records, and it had evolved a breed of musician whose professionalism was legendary. Studios were booked out in blocks of three hours, and it was expected that any given group of musicians would be able to set up their equipment, learn and record at least four songs in any one session.

Nashville's unique musical culture was complemented by its recording facilities. Since the earliest days of music recording, all four major cities had evolved different conventions over studio design, recording technique and equipment. Every studio would have its share of home-made equipment, and engineers would learn that city's approach to recording, based on trying to achieve the best sound with the rooms and the gear available to them. By the late 60s, top artists like Dylan or The Rolling Stones were free to travel to their studio of choice, but the same was not true of most recording engineers. The idea that a mere engineer could be a freelance, not bound by contract to a particular studio, was in its infancy, while the cross-pollination and eventual globalisation of recording techniques was years away.

In the 60s it was highly unusual for an engineer trained in one city to have any contact at all with studios elsewhere. Many American man-hours were spent puzzling over the sources of the "British Sound", while engineers in London were equally fixated on the records coming out of New York or Memphis. Even today, when you can find the same equipment and the same recording techniques in every studio in the world, Nashville retains a certain individuality. "When I first recorded in London I was amazed at how different the studios were and they were amazed at how different my approach was about recording," says Elliot Mazer, who recorded and produced the bulk of the material on *Harvest*. "Nashville studios were built to get solid tight rhythm sounds and isolated vocals. They had good earphone systems and good-sounding echo. New York and LA studios were mostly medium or large rooms that worked well for jazz groups and big pop records, and the studios and engineers thumbed their noses at rock."

In 1971, times were just beginning to change, and Elliot Mazer was in the vanguard. Nearly all Nashville studios were owned and staffed by Nashville people, but Mazer was from New York, where he had begun his career in the early 60s as an A & R man for Prestige Records. Unusually, although he was a capable recording engineer, he'd been a record producer first, working on a lot of jazz and folk records and learning about recording technique from some of the best-known studio wizards in New York. As a producer, he'd had the opportunities to travel that were denied to most engineers, and had first visited Nashville in 1963. "I loved the feeling down there," he says. "The studios were great for rhythm sections, the sound was fantastic and the musicians were amazing."

Impressed, Mazer had eventually decided to settle in Nashville. "I started to engineer my own records when I began doing projects in Nashville," he explains. "The engineers in Nashville were good, but they were more limited in their scope as they had only recorded country and some R & B. In New York I got to work with engineers like Rudy Van Gelder, Bob Fine, George Piros, Bill Blachly, Fred Catero, Fred Plaut, Frank Laico, Joe Tarsia and many others as a producer, before I went to Nashville. Down there I learned from the guys at Bradley's Barn and some of the classic engineers at RCA and Columbia. I prefer working with a good engineer, but after a while, I wanted to use some of the ideas that I learned in New York in Nashville and the best way to do that was to do it myself."

The resulting combination of Mazer's New York engineering training and Nashville musical profession-alism would, eventually, reach the ears of Neil Young and many other West Coast musicians. Mazer recorded some instrumental sessions with bassist Wayne Moss, drummer Kenny Buttrey and sundry other session regu-lars. This band eventually took the name Area Code 615, and their album would become very influential in the burgeoning country-rock scene.

"I did a few projects at Wayne Moss' Cinderella Sound and Wayne let me engineer and I let him play bass," explains Mazer. "That room was a two-car garage and it sounded great. The Area Code 615 projects were done there. That experience taught me a lot about recording."

Mazer soon decided to build a studio of his own: "David Briggs, Norbert Putnam and I built Quadrafonic Studios around this time. We wanted to build a slightly bigger room that gave us a lot of control and sounded tight and fat like Cinderella. I had the opportunity to do a lot of my own engineering there." Mazer's partners in the project were record producer Norbert Putnam and session pianist David Briggs (not the same David Briggs who had produced *After The Goldrush*). Thirty years later Mazer would be called upon to remix *Harvest* in surround sound, but at that time, engineers and producers were still getting to grips with stereo. "We called it Quadrafonic as a joke," says Mazer, "although it did have four speakers in the control room. I did one quad mix there."

The differences between Nashville and LA or New York weren't just musical: they were political. To his audience, Neil Young was a figure of the hippy counter-culture. The Buffalo Springfield had been prime movers in the alternative LA scene, embracing its drug culture and opposition to established authority. CSNY's very existence seemed to be a political statement, their every utterance scrutinised for its significance by fans and journalists. When four students were killed at Kent State University in 1970, Young documented his horror in 'Ohio'. Recorded by CSNY and rush-released within a month of the event, the resulting hit single was an unequivocal and powerful protest. Then, of course, there was 'Southern Man', Young's polemic against Southern racism and the Ku Klux Klan.

But country music was the music of the Southern Man, and there was little in common between the country world-view and the hippy outlook. The hippies were anti-establishment: country music *was* an establishment, and one that was strongly allied with forces of conservatism. Country songwriters might romanticise the plight of the soldier, but not because they were opposed to the Vietnam war. Sensitive hippies at least paid lip-service to the rise of feminism; with a few exceptions such as the remarkable Loretta Lynn, country music championed traditional, paternalistic family values. Even walking around with long hair was likely to get men beaten up in parts of the South, while open drug use was unheard of. Hippies and country music fans eyed one another from a great distance, with deep and mutual suspicion.

Embracing country music was thus a brave decision for someone who was a hero of the counter-culture, an icon of radical thought and politics. At least, it was when Bob Dylan did it.

Dylan already had a track record for upsetting his fans, having caused consternation among serious young men when he "went electric" in 1965. His decision to cast aside The Hawks and use Nashville session musicians to back him on 1966's *Blonde On Blonde* must have seemed equally perverse, although there was little on the album that sounded "country". It was the professionalism of the musicians that had impressed Dylan and producer Bob Johnston: Nashville's finest had almost certainly never been faced with an epic like 'Sad-Eyed Lady Of The Lowlands' before, but they had no trouble picking it up and playing it, straight off the bat.

Having recovered from a near-fatal motorbike crash, Dylan spent much of 1967 recording with his live band. The results, universally known as the *Basement Tapes*, were widely circulated in the music business as a catalogue of new Dylan songs for other artists to record, but he chose not to make them available to the public. Instead, he returned to Nashville to make an album of new material called *John Wesley Harding*. The recordings were stark and unadorned, while the material bore a clear country influence.

Dylan's next album went even further. It was not only recorded in Nashville, but named after the city. It boasted a duet with Johnny Cash, perhaps the biggest star in country music. Dylan's songwriting had also undergone a seismic shift. Grandiose allegories and clever wordplay had given way to simple, almost banal lyrics, and the harsh musical landscape of *Blonde On Blonde* had softened to the point where Dylan's singing actually sounded tuneful. *Nashville Skyline* was not the first or the best meeting of pop and country traditions, but it was by far the most important. It was also the first to be a hit.

Bob Dylan was not the only pop artist to be ahead of his audience in liking country music. The West Coast cognoscenti got turned on to bands like the aforementioned Area Code 615, whose popularity was boosted by the fact that Kenny Buttrey had drummed on Dylan's albums. Artists like Johnny Cash and Merle Haggard had plenty of admirers in the wider music business, and there were points of contact between country and hippy ideologies. Self-important rock stars craved the air of authenticity that surrounded country, its status as an American folk music. Johnny Cash was seen as the champion of the downtrodden and the outcast, and also had a drug intake that any self-respecting pop star would struggle to match. Meanwhile, other country stars were struggling to break the yoke of artistic control exercised by record company bosses, and looked enviously at the pop stars who were free to make the records they wanted to.

Like many others in the hippy movement, Neil Young was appalled by racism and the other problems that blighted the American South. However, Young seems never to have felt the almost instinctive distaste for country music and its culture that others, such as David Crosby, had to overcome. Young had grown up in Canada, where there was no civil rights struggle, no bitter legacy of Civil War division and slavery. Country radio had come crackling through the ether over the Great Plains just as had pop stations and rock 'n' roll shows. All went to make up Young's childhood musical education. As a good hippy, he would protest indignantly about prejudice and injustice in the South, yet he was never the kind of rock star who would flinch at the sound of a pedal steel guitar. The gut-rooted association between country music and redneck politics never seems to have taken hold in Young.

By the time Neil Young made it to Nashville, the idea of a counter-culture rock star collaborating with the redneck enemy had lost some of its political significance. *Nashville Skyline* was almost two years old, and its impact had been followed up by the likes of The Band. The city itself was becoming recognised as a place where musicians got things done, quickly and well, and artists of all shapes and sizes were flying there to record. Rock and country were beginning to build a shared audience thanks to syndicated TV extravaganzas like *The Johnny*

Cash Show, which showcased country's biggest acts alongside the likes of Dylan, Joni Mitchell and James Taylor.

Although it could still provoke ill-feeling, in 1971 it was no longer automatically assumed that a pop star going to Nashville was about to become a poster child for the Republicans — in Young's case, that wouldn't happen for another ten years. Nor did it necessarily mean that he would come back with an album of country music. It could, however, be a comment on the state of rock music. Dylan's alignment with the Nashville music industry was a deliberate reaction against the more complex, experimental approach to record production that was becoming commonplace in pop and rock music. The Beatles' *Sergeant Pepper's Lonely Hearts Club Band* had triggered this rash of studio experimentation on its 1967 release. Many found it inspiring, but Bob Dylan was not among them. "I thought *Sergeant Pepper* was a very indulgent album," he later said. "I didn't think all that production was necessary."

Neil Young had contributed to his fair share of "studio as an instrument" recordings. Buffalo Springfield's most ambitious pieces, such as 'Broken Arrow' and 'Expecting To Fly', were Young compositions, elaborately layered and edited. His first solo album was similarly dense with overdubs and effects, while Crosby, Stills and Nash became a byword for studio excess. With *After*

The Goldrush, however, Young had turned decisively against this approach.

If Dylan went back to basics in the studio as a protest against rock star egotism, Neil Young's motivation seems to have been less high-minded. No rock star who chose to record with the London Symphony Orchestra could be too concerned to avoid accusations of self-indulgence, yet Young stuck to his new-found philosophy of recording even then, singing and playing live as the orchestra sawed away. The simple truth seems to be that Young felt he made better records that way. Young had struggled to find musicians in LA who shared his ideals, and had largely failed to persuade Crosby, Stills and Nash to do so. In Nashville, it was the way records had always been made.

Nevertheless, when Young made his first visit there, he did so with no firm intention to record an album. The visit itself was the result of the mellowing relations between pop and country: Young had been invited to appear on *The Johnny Cash Show*, alongside Linda Ronstadt, James Taylor and Tony Joe White. He probably wasn't expecting to acquire a new band and a new producer at the same time.

Recording Harvest

With contacts from his New York days, Elliot Mazer was able to act as a bridge between Nashville and the rest of the world. One of these contacts was Neil Young's manager, Elliot Roberts, who also managed Joni Mitchell. Young's fellow guest artists on *The Johnny Cash Show* included singer Linda Ronstadt, who Elliot Mazer also knew, having produced her *Silk Purse* LP. Knowing that Roberts, Young and Ronstadt were coming to Nashville, Mazer invited them and the other *Cash Show* guests to a dinner party.

Neil Young and Elliot Mazer fell to talking, and Young revealed that he had some new material he was hoping to record. He was familiar with the Area Code 615 albums, and asked Mazer whether he could get the band's rhythm section and steel player into the studio the next day to accompany him.

Although drummer Kenny Buttrey was available, bassist Norbert Putnam and pedal steel player Weldon Myrick had other commitments. Fortunately, good musicians were in plentiful supply in Nashville, and a band was swiftly assembled comprising Buttrey, songwriter Troy Seals on bass and session guitarist Teddy Irwin. Seals' place was soon taken by Tim Drummond, who'd been told about the session that afternoon, and the band was completed by pedal steel guitarist Ben Keith. Young brought with him a freak Nashville snowstorm.

"When Neil played those songs, everything about the arrangements and sound seemed obvious," recalls Elliot. "Neil was totally prepared with songs when he got to the studio. The songs were great and he had the feels and the basic arrangements worked out.

"Neil came in, sang the songs and looked at the studio. We set up the studio so that he could be right in between the members of the band. He asked if we could put him near the drums. I brought him in for his first playback and he was happy, and off we went. We had great sounds, great earphone mixes and we were ready to go a few minutes after he got to the studio. The studio never got in his way.

"Quad was a two-storey Victorian-era house. The control room was the porch, the playing rooms were the living room and the dining room which were connected by sliding doors. The living room had wood panels and was [acoustically] lively, the dining room was padded. Neil sat between the rooms in the doorway. Kenny was in the living room to his left and the rest were to his right — bass, steel, piano, second guitar, banjo."

This arrangement, with all the musicians in the same room, was not so far removed from the approach Young and David Briggs had adopted on *After The Goldrush*. Although each instrument had its own microphone and would have its own track on the 16-track recorder, it meant there was no way of maintaining absolute isolation. The sound of drums was bound to creep on to everything, while it would be impossible to maintain complete aural separation between all the instruments crammed into the dining room. Elliot Mazer knew that this might lead to trouble at the mixing stage, but it was the only way to capture a true live performance: "The leakage gave the record character and we knew we were not going to replace anything."

Like Dylan and so many others, Young had been attracted by the idea of recording in Nashville at least partly because of the quality of that city's musicians. Now that he had corralled some of the finest session men in the world into a room, he laid down the law about how he wanted them to arrange his songs. In Crazy Horse, he'd found a band who were willing to back him in the most basic style imaginable, playing nothing that was not absolutely necessary to get the song across. In the case of Crazy Horse, this was largely because that was the only way they could play: they made a virtue of their lack of proficiency.

Nashville's session musicians were nothing if not proficient. Unlike Crosby, Stills and Nash, however, they were used to being treated as sidemen, never indulging in instrumental grandstanding unless that was what the client demanded. For the *Harvest* sessions, Young went in the opposite direction, insisting on the simplest of arrangements. It was almost as though he was trying to reduce these hugely talented and experienced players to the level of Crazy Horse. "Neil's songs dictated the arrangements," says Elliot Mazer. "We asked Kenny to not play any fills on some songs and no hi-hat on another. One on song he sat on his right hand."

The musicians Young and Mazer had assembled were professional enough to fulfil these demands to the letter, but doing so didn't make them sound like Crazy Horse. The Horse had displayed more subtlety in the *After The Goldrush* sessions than they had on *Everybody Knows This Is Nowhere*, but they were still fundamentally a garage band, constantly in danger of dropping the beat or fluffing a chord change. With The Stray Gators, as the new collection of musicians would eventually be known, things worked on a different level. Even though Young was placing severe limits on their freedom to interpret his material, they were able to use their experience and ability in countless small ways. "Kenny is a fantastic drummer," says Elliot Mazer by way of explanation. "He was great playing right with Neil, catching accents and making the songs come alive."

One significant difference between the *Harvest* band and any of Young's previous groups was the presence of Ben Keith on pedal steel guitar. Young's bare-bones arrangements on songs like 'Out On The Weekend' boldly left acres of open space, and Ben Keith's playing did not so much fill these open spaces as emphasise their presence. His thin chords skirted around the edges of the songs, pointing up the sparseness of the music rather than padding it out. Keith would become one of Young's most constant musical collaborators in years to come, and it's easy to see why.

Other singers are described as having brassy or reedy singing voices, and it doesn't seem too fanciful to describe Neil Young as having a pedal-steely voice. Young's confidence in his singing had drastically improved since his Buffalo Springfield days, and its distinctiveness was only enhanced by his policy of recording everything live. Mournful, high-pitched, keening, never quite in tune, it was matched perfectly by the sound of pedal steel, to which all the same adjectives could be applied. Even *Rolling Stone*'s damning review had to admit that, on *Harvest*, "Neil Young still sings awful pretty", and the album contains some of his finest vocal performances.

For the first Nashville session in February 1971, Young also called on the services of his fellow *Cash Show* guests James Taylor and Linda Ronstadt. Their introduction to Young's recording methods took the form of a short, sharp shock. For the recording of 'Old Man', Taylor was handed a six-string banjo, an instrument he'd never played before, while the pair contributed backing vocals in a rather more offhand manner than they were used to. Mazer threw up a microphone in the control room, Taylor and Ronstadt sang along, and that was that.

"Each song was cut in a few takes," says Elliot Mazer. "With Neil, you can tell from the start if a take is going to be magic. He lets that happen when he feels the band and the studio are ready. All of Neil's sessions feel like the music he is recording, and these sessions were warm and friendly. They had a great feel to them. The sessions felt like the way the music sounded."

This first session lasted a weekend and yielded *Harvest*'s two hit singles 'Heart Of Gold' and 'Old Man'. A third song, 'Bad Fog Of Loneliness', was also recorded, but would not make it to the final track listing and remains unreleased. "That song did not stand up to the others," says Elliot Mazer. "It fell out the race early."

It was immediately obvious to both Mazer and Kenny Buttrey that 'Heart Of Gold' was destined to be a hit. Neil Young too was excited about the results of his first Nashville recording session, and what plans he might have had for a live album were shelved for good. According to his biographer Jimmy McDonough, Young was so taken with the Quadrafonic recordings that he didn't even listen to the tapes of the concerts he'd had recorded in Toronto.

Two songs, of course, were not enough to make an album, and a second session at Quadrafonic was booked, with the same musicians, for early April. In the meantime, Young was due to visit London to play at the Royal Festival Hall and record a solo live session for BBC TV's *The Old Grey Whistle Test*. Most of the songs Young played for the BBC's invited audience were new, and several would end up on *Harvest*. 'Out On The Weekend' was so new that he forgot the words.

He and Jack Nitzsche used the rest of their time in London to record the two songs for which Nitzsche had written orchestral arrangements. 'A Man Needs A Maid' and 'There's A World' were both cut in the Assembly Hall at Barking Town Hall with the London Symphony Orchestra. Young sang and played piano live, while hot-shot engineer Glyn Johns manned the controls in the Rolling Stones mobile truck. (Located in an unprepossessing suburb of East London, the Assembly Hall doesn't sound like an obvious choice. It is, however, one of a number of out-of-the-way London halls that is highly regarded for its acoustics, and has often been used for orchestral recordings: it was a favourite of cult soundtrack composer Bernard Herrmann, who recorded many of his film scores there.)

According to the liner notes for Young's *Decade* compilation, the London trip also yielded a new song. 'Harvest' would eventually provide the title for his album, and was one of the songs Young and The Stray Gators tackled on his return to Quadrafonic. Once again, Elliot Mazer engineered and sat in the producer's chair; and once again, a weekend's work yielded masters for two songs, 'Out On The Weekend' and 'Harvest'. Attempts to record another song, 'Alabama', were not so successful. Young realised that this, and another new song, 'Words', needed more muscle than he could provide in his enforced sitting-down acoustic mode.

Young's back problems persisted, and he became increasingly frustrated with both the medication he was forced to take and his inability to play an electric guitar. Eventually, in August 1971, he had surgery to remove some discs from his back, and returned to his ranch to recuperate. The following month, Elliot Mazer and The Stray Gators joined him there, where they would complete *Harvest*. The band set up in an old barn full of bird shit, and a Wally Heider remote recording truck was hired to immortalise their output. Quadrafonic Studios had proved perfect for capturing the mellow feel of songs like 'Heart Of Gold', but it was a less ideal environment for recording noisier material. " 'Words', 'Alabama' and 'Are You Ready For The Country' needed to be cut in a big room," says Elliot Mazer. "We had cut a quiet version of 'Alabama' at Quadrafonic, but it was not as good as the one we cut at the ranch." The DVD-A version of *Harvest* boasts a short film clip of Mazer "behind the barn" explaining how he set up microphones outdoors to record a fortuitous natural echo created by the shape of the land and buildings.

The photo on the back cover of *Harvest*, taken by Neil Young's archivist Joel Bernstein, shows The Stray Gators at work in the barn on Young's ranch, where they were augmented by Jack Nitzsche. The intention was that Nitzsche would play piano, as the session men who'd tinkled the ivories on 'Harvest' and 'Old Man' had remained in Nashville. This he did, but Young also repeated the trick he'd played on Nils Lofgren. Lofgren was a talented guitarist, and Young had forced him to play piano: now pianist Nitzsche was inveigled into playing slide guitar on 'Are You Ready For The Country'. Young himself had recovered from the operation enough to stand up and play a Gretsch White Falcon electric guitar instead of the acoustic he'd been forced to use for the previous year or so.

This time, backing vocal duties were undertaken by
Young's more established collaborators Stephen Stills,
David Crosby and Graham Nash. Nash's stay provided
one of the more famous stories of Neil Young's eccen-
tricity, when the Englishman received a sneak preview
of the new album in a rowing boat on the lake that lay
behind the barn. Young and Mazer had set up a giant
outdoor stereo system, with one stack of speakers in
the barn and another in Young's house. When Mazer
came and stood on the shore to ask how it sounded,
Young yelled back "More barn!" You can get an idea
of the size of the sound rig from the interview with
Young on the *Harvest* DVD, where a playback of
'Words' rings out across the hills.

'Words', 'Alabama' and 'Are You Ready For The
Country' were duly completed, and *Harvest*'s track list-
ing was bulked out by the two orchestral pieces Young
had completed with Jack Nitzsche and a fragment from
the aborted live album. On January 30, 1971, the final
American date of Neil Young's solo tour had taken
him to Royce Hall at the University of California, Los
Angeles, where it was taped by Henry Lewy in a Wally
Heider mobile truck. One song from this concert, 'The
Needle And The Damage Done', wound up on *Harvest*.
"No other Royce Hall recordings were considered,"
says Elliot Mazer. "Neil chose that one. Neil has a

phenomenal memory and he can recall a particular take from years before."

Once the track listing had been decided, Young and Elliot Mazer set about mixing the album at Young's ranch. On the title track, no mixing was necessary: the stereo master they'd recorded at the time was deemed good enough to use. The other songs, however, needed a fair amount of work. "Trying to recapture the feeling of the original sessions was the challenge," says Mazer. Despite the lengthy mixing process, the results have a straightforward, pure quality to them. Most pop and rock records make use of a technique known as compression to even out the level of the different elements in a mix. This can give individual instruments and voices a thicker and more substantial sound, but if over-used it can also leave recordings sounding flat and lacking in dynamics. Elliot Mazer deliberately avoided using compression anywhere on *Harvest*, and the resulting sound is open and spacious.

The idea that Young had "gone country" was reinforced by Tom Wilkes' sleeve design. The cover of *After The Goldrush* had seen Young lurking anonymously in a grey city street: here, the only image was a red disc, around which Young's name and the album title flowed in elaborate calligraphy. With its muted buff background, the results had a decidedly rustic air. Nowhere on *Harvest* did Young's face appear clearly: although Joel Bernstein's black and white photo for the back cover showed The Stray Gators getting down in the barn, Young was just a mess of hair. The inside of the gatefold sleeve was even more obscure, a blurred, distorted Neil Young reflected in a polished brass doorknob. It was easier to decipher the words by listening to the record than by struggling with Young's handwriting, but the lyric sheet was a thoughtful finishing touch. As a package, *Harvest* was understated, nicely crafted, touchingly self-effacing. It was a fine cover for what Young would come to see as his finest album.

Harvest Time

Harvest is the only Neil Young album that has found its way into the record collections of people who don't have record collections. For every person who's become a Neil Young fan after buying it, there are probably twenty who have ignored every other album he's ever made.

In any given year, there will be a handful of albums that snowball to multi-platinum sales not because they appeal to music fans, but because they somehow strike a chord with the casual listener. It's relatively easy to sell records to people who read the music papers with religious fervour and spend every Saturday afternoon thumbing through record-store racks. The trouble is that there aren't enough of them. The Holy Grail for record companies is not the kind of album that achieves rave reviews and the admiration of the chin-stroking brigade, but the kind of album that is bought by people who buy one album a year.

After the fact, it seems obvious that such albums were always going to be commercial smashes. It's rather less easy to predict in advance which two or three of the thousands of albums released every year will do the business, even more difficult for record companies to know which artists will deliver such an album in three or five or ten years' time, and absolutely impossible to find a formula that will produce a hit album on demand. Thanks in large measure to his bullish manager Elliot Roberts, Neil Young had been able to pursue his solo career with very little artistic "direction" from the record company. If he wanted to ping-pong between hard rock and folk music, he could; he could make music with a symphony orchestra or a garage band and they would happily pick up the tab. *Harvest* justified Warner Bros' faith in him, while some of his subsequent albums would try that faith to its limits.

"I'm convinced that what I do and what sells are two completely different things," Young told Cameron Crowe in 1975. "If they meet, it's coincidence." Coincidence, in this case, hit the nail on the head. The first single from *Harvest*, 'Heart Of Gold', was released in February 1972, picked up by FM radio and propelled to the top of the singles chart in Britain and the USA. The album too moved rapidly to the No. 1 slot on both sides of the Atlantic and stayed there, eventually becoming the best-selling album of 1972 and, in later years, one of Warner Bros' most reliable back-catalogue warhorses.

From the critical consensus of the 1970s, you might think that this had been Neil Young's only aim in making *Harvest*. Some writers made it seem as though Young cynically set out to do whatever would sell the most copies, without a thought for artistic invention or integrity. This was nonsense then and now. If there's one thing that Young's career has demonstrated beyond doubt, it's that he couldn't make a consciously commercial album if his life depended upon it. When he's followed a trend, it's because he believed in the musicians who were leading it. He was, for instance, one of very few 60s survivors to engage creatively with punk rock in the late 70s, and perhaps the only one to come out of it with his reputation enhanced. When his then label Geffen pressured him to update his sound in the 80s, they got the baffling *Trans* and the flops *Landing On Water* and *Life*.

Harvest took a year to make, but not because Young was meticulously polishing its every phrase to some peak of commercial smoothness. By the increasingly indulgent standards of the 70s, the sessions were remarkably brief: a short trip to London, a couple of weekends in Nashville and a few weeks on Young's ranch. The album was not laid down according to some overarching master plan, but pieced together like a patchwork, the track listing added to whenever Young was able to snatch a few days of studio time. Where bands like Steely Dan forged their best-selling albums by painstaking studio work, layering overdub after over-dub to create a flawless, slick production, Young insisted on recording everything live. Whatever he thought he was doing by flying Nashville's finest session men to California and having them play in a broken-down barn, it wasn't "selling out".

Nevertheless, *Harvest* caught the public imagination in a way no other Young album has achieved. What gave it this universal appeal? Young's own explanation gets to the heart of the matter: *Harvest* may not be a work of art, but it is a very fine album. In particular, it's one of few Neil Young albums in which solid, tradi-tional, old-fashioned songwriting craft is the central feature. Young imposed his own sensibilities on the Nashville sound, yet The Stray Gators' musicianship is complemented by melodies and chord changes that any hack songwriter would kill for.

Prior to *Harvest*, Young's songwriting had veered between two extremes. At one lay pieces like 'The Old Laughing Lady' and Buffalo Springfield's 'Broken Arrow', which saw him striving too hard for lyrical depth and musical sophistication. Equally cerebral were

Dylanesque folk numbers such as 'Sugar Mountain' and 'I Am A Child', hamstrung by precious turns of phrase and uptight guitar picking. At the other extreme, Young's work with Crazy Horse was positively skeletal. Songs like 'Down By The River' and 'Round And Round' seemed to exist only as frames for lengthy jams.

On *After The Goldrush*, Young's breakthrough album, he reached a fertile middle ground. Songs like 'I Believe In You' and 'Don't Let It Bring You Down' showed Young's folkie sensibility ruthlessly purged of lyrical and musical indulgence, allowing space for powerful, expressive performances. Rockers such as 'When You Dance' retained the freshness of 'Down By The River' but never degenerated into endless jams. Only 'Tell My Why' still sagged under precious lyrics and over-elaborate guitar playing: more often, the songs suffered from being too simple, like the dirge that was 'Birds'. As an album, *After The Goldrush* boasted good enough tunes to overcome any excessive minimalism on the part of its creator. Young had stripped his songs and his sound back to the bare essentials, and the results had vindicated him.

Compared to *After The Goldrush*, *Harvest* seems more refined, for several reasons. Firstly, there's the sound of the album. Recording *After The Goldrush* in a basement studio had been a remarkable achievement, yet the results inevitably have a very dry, direct sound:

producer David Briggs had had no means of adding echo to any of the instruments. The Nashville material on *Harvest*, by contrast, was laid down in a purpose-designed studio, and boasts a different kind of smoothness and warmth, while the tracks recorded in the barn and at Barking Town Hall have the expansiveness that comes of recording in a larger space.

Secondly, there's The Stray Gators' contribution. All of Young's determination to impose a minimalist aesthetic on his musicians could not prevent their class from showing through. There are no virtuoso performances on *Harvest*, but when Kenny Buttrey plays a boom-tish drum part, it sounds different from one of Ralph Molina's. The album is full of little touches of sophistication, like Teddy Irwin's guitar harmonics and Buttrey's deft hi-hat rhythm in 'Heart Of Gold'. Ben Keith's pedal steel provides the perfect counterpoint to Young's voice, which is presented here at its very sweetest.

Most importantly, there are the songs themselves. Many of the critics who disliked *Harvest* at the time of its release accused Young of treading water. It was, they suggested, just a rehash of his previous album, lacking in new ideas or focus. Looking back at both albums in the context of Young's later career, this does not seem a fair criticism. 'Alabama' certainly revisited the same lyrical theme as the earlier 'Southern Man', but it's hard to see why that should make it redundant, or why the rest of the album should be tarred with the same brush. *After The Goldrush* and *Harvest* each has its own, distinctive voice; and one can trace a clear line of development in Young's songwriting between the two.

When he wrote the songs that would appear on *After The Goldrush*, Young eliminated much of the complexity and cleverness he'd employed on his solo debut. On *Harvest*, he allowed some of it to return: but this time, he was better able to master it. 'Out On The Weekend' and 'Old Man', for instance, retain the core virtues of catchy melody and memorable lyrics, yet these are supported by guitar arrangements that go far beyond up-and-down strumming. The broken chords and delicate picking patterns are not decorative but central to the composition. There's not a note in either that doesn't absolutely need to be there, but at the same time, neither song could stand to be reduced to the level of 'Round And Round'.

For all of the finesse that's evident on songs like 'Old Man', however, few people would suggest that *Harvest* is a better album than *After The Goldrush*. It's flawed in ways its predecessor isn't, the most obvious criticism being that it's uneven. *Harvest* contains some of Neil Young's most enduring songs, but it also contains songs that are difficult to make sense of, songs so basic they might have been written in minutes, and at least one turkey that escaped quality control. It's proof, if proof were wanted, that a classic album need not be uniform, or uniformly good.

The charge of inconsistency can be levelled at most of Neil Young's albums, including those that are beloved of critics and fans. If you like Neil Young, you get used to the idea that his albums rarely mine a single stylistic vein throughout. On his best albums, the different facets of his musical personality work together to create a varied yet musically satisfying whole. *Harvest* is one of Young's most eclectic albums, showcasing almost all of the different musical characters he'd evolved in his solo career. The price of this diversity is that the album develops through a series of abrupt stylistic jumps, rather than by evolving and building an overarching mood. The weaker songs on *After The Goldrush* are carried off by the feel of the album as a whole, but each song on *Harvest* is left to stand or fall on its own merits. For every sympathetic pairing of two songs, there's another juxtaposition that feels awkward or unnatural.

This is ultimately frustrating, but at the same time, it goes some way to explaining why *Harvest* is a compelling album to listen to, why we want to hear it over and over again. For all the mellowness in evidence, the listener is kept slightly on edge; our expectations are built up and then undercut. The individual tracks are not musically "difficult" but as they're presented on *Harvest*, they form a surprisingly difficult album. We expect to be able to experience an album as some sort of linear narrative, but *Harvest* resists any attempt to impose one. The songs are slight enough to be grasped the first time you hear them, yet the thread that binds them together remains elusive even on repeated listening. We play it again because we want to "get" *Harvest*, to find out what links the pieces of the puzzle; but the best we can do is glimpse fragments of a solution.

The first two songs, 'Out On The Weekend' and 'Harvest', work together to create a pleasantly melancholic mood. Then, just when you've got used to the wistful sound of Country Neil, Epic Neil appears from nowhere with the London Symphony Orchestra in tow. The orchestral arrangement for 'A Man Needs A Maid' might not seem overblown if it was presented in isolation, but it does following the down-home simplicity of 'Harvest'. Together, the charming, impossibly catchy 'Heart Of Gold' and the poignant 'Old Man' could have restored the atmosphere, but here they're separated by a mediocre country-blues jam, not to mention the break between sides one and two.

Harvest's eclecticism is even more pronounced in the second half. It's harder to give Epic Neil the benefit of the doubt when you've heard the delicate 'Old Man' give way to the ill-judged bombast of 'There's A World'. Then, without warning, we discover that Neil Young is going to rock out after all, and do it in style. 'Alabama' is a great piece of menacing rock music, good enough to erase the memory of the preceding song; but no sooner has Young's ragged electric guitar died away than we are thrown by another of *Harvest*'s twists. Any idea that the album might be building to some sort of climax is undercut by the subdued tones of Young the folk troubadour, gravely lecturing his audience on the evils of heroin. Before they can even finish applauding him, however, everything is washed away in the churning tide of 'Words', endless waves of guitar eddying around fragments of incomprehensible verse.

Despite its diversity, *Harvest* was quickly pigeonholed by the press and the public in a way that previous Neil Young albums hadn't been. The fact that Young had visited Nashville to record was widely publicised, and the album's cover art did nothing to undermine the perception that Neil Young had "gone country". Bob Dylan's *Nashville Skyline* had acted like a rock cast into a pool: by the time *Harvest* was released, the waves had spread to every shore, country-rock was the flavour of the month, and Young reaped the rewards. Most influential of all in shaping the image of *Harvest* was Young's first major hit single. With its prominent pedal steel part and backing vocals from country-rock queen Linda Ronstadt, 'Heart Of Gold' seemed to signal a clear change of direction for Young, in the same way that 'Lay Lady Lay' had for Dylan.

It is, of course, not unknown for an album to hit on the strength of a completely uncharacteristic single. Many of those who bought The Zombies' *Odessey & Oracle* on the strength of 'Time Of The Season', for example, were surprised to hear very little sweaty R & B and a lot of pastoral psychedelia. Yet while no one song could be considered truly typical of *Harvest*, 'Heart Of Gold' was probably as representative as any. No style could be said to dominate the album, but Country Neil is definitely the most prominent.

In truth, however, *Harvest* doesn't engage very deeply with country music. Pioneers of country-rock such as The Byrds and The Flying Burrito Brothers had gone much further than Young, dressing in rhinestones, cowboy boots and stetsons, and placing their own compositions alongside standards from Merle Haggard and The Louvin Brothers. Compared to *Sweetheart Of The Rodeo* or *The Gilded Palace Of Sin*, *Harvest* is hardly a genre-defining album. Nashville had left its stamp on the way *Harvest* sounded, but at heart it was a collection of Neil Young songs, not an album of country songs.

The rustic cover art suggests countrification, as does the presence of a pedal steel guitar, a Nashville pick-up band and a song called 'Are You Ready For The

Country?', but any country element in the music itself is largely superficial. Other than on the title track, the core features of country music — its typical chord sequences, rhythms, song structures and "dum dum" bass lines — are notably only by their absence. A few pedal steel licks do not make *Harvest* a country album, any more than the violins and timpani make it a symphonic one.

Harvest succeeded partly because it had the trappings of a country album, but not much of the content. It was country and western for people who didn't like country and western, who couldn't stomach the real deal. For many hardcore fans, *Harvest* is flawed for a similar reason: it's Neil Young for people who don't like Neil Young. It represents a kind of Neil Young Lite, watering down his emotional intensity to the point where it is palatable to the masses.

To some extent, this perception is just a consequence of *Harvest*'s success. Fans are a perverse lot, often expressing attachment to their chosen artist's most obscure and difficult work purely because it is obscure and difficult. Beach Boys acolytes turn up a united nose at *Beach Boys Party* while engaging in furious debates over the track listing for *Smile*. Vienna in 1801 was probably full of serious-faced young men muttering that the Moonlight Sonata was a sell-out for Beethoven, and what you really needed was the bootleg score of the unreleased Black Piano Concerto. *Harvest* is almost too easy to like, and doing so opens the Neil Young devotee up to the charge of being lightweight, of having only a casual interest in their subject. Likewise, no rock critic could call it Young's best album and retain the respect of his or her peers. What, after all, is the point in a rock critic who simply agrees with the record-buying public?

Harvest's good qualities have, all too often, been ignored. It has many virtues: strong tunes, artfully artless arrangements, and great performances, especially from Young himself. Perhaps its best feature is that it never becomes boring: even when you're aware of its faults, you don't want to stop listening to it. I must have put it on a hundred times while writing this book, and I'm not sick of it yet.

In the final analysis, however, it is hard to deny that the fans and critics have a point. *Harvest* may have virtues that are completely absent from Young's best albums, but it misses something that is ultimately more significant than melody or finesse: substance. 'A Man Needs A Maid' is the only song on *Harvest* with the emotional weight of 'Tonight's The Night' or 'I Believe In You', and Young chose to bury it behind an avalanche of orchestration. Elsewhere, as on 'Old Man' and 'Heart Of Gold', Young refined his songwriting technique to perfection, yet the results remain more the product of craft than art. *Harvest* has more pretty tunes and neat turnarounds than any other record in Young's catalogue, but it lacks the gut-wrenching impact of his best work. It is, as Neil Young said, a fine album, but Neil Young has made great albums.

After Harvest

Having put himself in the middle of the road, according to the myth, Neil Young responded by heading for the ditch. It's undoubtedly true that for the rest of the 70s, coincidence would not bring together what he did and what sold. While it's a mistake to damn *Harvest* as overly commercial in intent, though, it's also missing the point to see his subsequent career as a bloody-minded exercise in alienating the audience that album had won him.

Of course the success of *Harvest* affected Young profoundly: how could it not? He was already uneasy about celebrity and the idea of being a "rich hippy", and it would make him a whole lot richer and a whole lot more famous. *Harvest* certainly didn't leave him craving attention. He disliked being a public figure and, as he would explain in 'Don't Be Denied' from *Time Fades Away*, hated the thought of being "a millionaire through a businessman's eyes". People he'd thought were his friends now appeared intent on taking money from him. The same band that had happily clattered away in a barn to create *Harvest* became involved in bitter arguments about their share of the cash when Young took them on tour. "I thought the record was good," he later told Cameron Crowe, "but I also knew that something else was dying. I became very reclusive."

Young also seems to have been stung by the attitude of the rock critics. He took a swipe at the profession in 'Ambulance Blues' from his 1974 album *On The Beach*, declaiming

So all you critics sit alone
You're no better than me from what you've shown
With your stomach pump and your hook-and-ladder dreams

John Mendelssohn claimed that Young was sufficiently incensed by his *Rolling Stone* review to show up at one of Mendelssohn's own concerts with the intention of humiliating him in public. Yet the critical reaction to *Harvest* cannot have been wholly responsible for Young's departure from the straight and narrow. It was, after all, hardly the first time Young had been on the receiving end of a negative review: his previous solo album *After The Goldrush* had also suffered a kicking within the pages of *Rolling Stone*, while a sense of disappointment had greeted the much-hyped Crosby, Stills, Nash and Young album *Déjà Vu* in some quarters.

The immense popularity Young had achieved with *Harvest* no doubt hardened his feelings about the emptiness of commercial success, but it did not produce those feelings out of nowhere. Young had always been ambivalent about stardom, even though he sought it with a drive and ruthlessness that often ruffled feathers. The perils of fame had inspired at least two of his songs from Buffalo Springfield days, 'Mr. Soul' and 'Broken Arrow', and his marriage to Susan Acevedo had suffered because of Young's inability to escape celebrity status. Before he even made *Harvest* he'd retreated into the wilds of California to try to get away from it all. The *Harvest* experience made Young even more reluctant to play the rock star, but it was circumstance rather than conscious effort that brought him into the ditch.

Repeating *Harvest*'s success with his next album would not have been easy, even if Neil Young really had become an evil commercial mastermind with no interest other than making money. As it was, his next album was a spectacular flop, but not because of any premeditated career sabotage on the part of Young himself.

Around the time *Harvest* was made, Young had been nursing a growing interest in film-making, and his next project was his debut feature-length movie *Journey*

Through The Past. Warner Bros agreed to distribute the film on condition that they could also release a soundtrack album. When they saw the film, they decided it was a lost cause and shelved it, but, eager for a follow-up to the best-selling *Harvest*, went ahead and released the double soundtrack album anyway. It contained just one new Young song, sandwiched between some weak concert recordings and fragments of music from the likes of The Beach Boys. It had only ever been intended as a soundtrack album; as the new LP by superstar Neil Young, it was a disaster.

Young was a little more culpable for his next sales disappointment, but again it was events outside his control that really hit home. To mark his hit album and the fact that his back had finally healed, he had Elliot Roberts book a huge tour. As 1972 drew to a close, with *Harvest* still riding high in the charts, Young assembled a band at the ranch to rehearse. To the core of The Stray Gators — Ben Keith, Tim Drummond and Kenny Buttrey — he added two further musicians, Jack Nitzsche and Danny Whitten. Young had been told that Whitten was now clean, but a few days' rehearsal on the ranch made clear that his drug-taking was worse than ever. Reluctantly, Neil Young bought him a plane ticket to Los Angeles, gave him 50 dollars and sent him on his way. He spent the money on drugs, overdosed, and died the same night in a friend's bathroom.

Whitten's death set the tone for a calamitous tour. Young's voice wasn't up to such a strenuous schedule, and he was never satisfied with the sound in the vast arenas he'd chosen to play in. Noting the colossal success of *Harvest*, the band members mutinied for more money, Buttrey eventually leaving to be replaced by Johnny Barbata. Young and Nitzsche began drinking heavily, and the performances became more and more ragged. What's more, his new material had little in common with the mellow *Harvest* sound: it was electric rock 'n' roll, noisier and with sharper edges.

The album that eventually emerged was a live album from the tour. Rather than containing rocked-up performances of familiar songs, however, *Time Fades Away* collected eight previously unreleased numbers. The band were sloppy, the mix was skewed, Young's voice sounded hoarse and out of tune, and the songs were either obtuse or painfully personal. It's possible that Young put it out as a deliberate attempt to distance himself from the middle of the road, but it seems much more likely that he was simply too exhausted to contemplate going into the studio and recording anything else. Either way, *Time Fades Away* was another difficult album to sell. If you could get past the roughness, it was also one of his most interesting, but it's not hard to see why it didn't fly off the shelves. Young would, wrongly, go on to describe it as his worst album, and ignored it completely when he put together his *Decade* compilation.

The sloppiness of *Time Fades Away* was an accurate reflection of Young and the band's condition during their marathon tour. For his next project, he achieved an even more extreme state of mind; and this time he did it on purpose. It's hard to imagine a much less commercial concept than *Tonight's The Night*. An extended, drunken wake for Danny Whitten and fellow drug victim Bruce Berry, the songs were taped late into the night, when Young and the band were so inebriated they could barely play. *Tonight's The Night* was very definitely not a "fine" album. In the event, its release was delayed almost two years while Young fine-tuned its running order to be as harrowing as possible, and Warner Bros heaved a collective gulp of anticipation.

Indeed, *Tonight's The Night* nearly wasn't released at all. Young had been planning to follow up *On The Beach*, another rather cheerless affair, with a collection of pleasant acoustic numbers called *Homegrown*. He had returned to Nashville and Quadrafonic to cut songs like 'Star Of Bethlehem', and the album promised a belated return to the mellow, accessible sound of *Harvest*. "*Homegrown* was the missing link between *Harvest*, *Comes A Time*, *Old Ways* and *Harvest Moon*," Young later told Jimmy McDonough. Young unveiled *Homegrown* to some friends at a drunken listening party: unfortunately for it, *Tonight's The Night* was on the same tape. After hearing them back to back, Young changed his mind and released *Tonight's The Night* instead. Most of the *Homegrown* material remains unreleased except on bootlegs.

Neil Young, it seemed, was not yet ready to play the MOR pop superstar again: or was he? On the one hand, he shelved a saleable album to release *Tonight's The Night*, in full expectation of poor reviews and worse sales. On the other, however, he was happy to hook up with Crosby, Stills and Nash once more. A projected second studio album failed to materialise, but the foursome embarked on the most lavish and lucrative tour in the history of rock music. The *Time Fades Away* tour had convinced Young that he didn't like playing in stadiums, yet here he was participating in the biggest stadium tour any rock band had yet attempted. Young had not completely lost interest in being a superstar or making money.

Neil Young would, eventually, return to the *Harvest* sound, or something like it, but it would not be this sound that brought him back into favour with the critics and the record-buying public. For his 1978 album *Comes A Time* he revisited Nashville to record another pleasant selection of country-tinged ballads, although the sparseness of *Harvest* was replaced by a lush backing involving frightening numbers of violinists. The album was moderately well-received, and sold healthily, but it was his next outing with Crazy Horse that would see him featured in almost everyone's "Best Albums Of 1979". *Rust Never Sleeps* offered a side of Folkie Neil, while side two introduced Punk Neil. Seven years after *Harvest*, what sold and what Neil Young did had caught up with one another again.

As if to prove that this was just coincidence, it would be another ten years before Young once again clambered back out of the ditch. In the early 80s, Young's contract with Warner Bros expired and he signed to Geffen Records. Here he came under greater pressure to produce hit albums, pressure which would culminate in an infamous episode where Geffen sued him for recording "uncharacteristic" material. The decade saw him adopt yet more new characters with increasing desperation — Electro Neil, Rockabilly Neil, Pop Neil, even Blues Neil — but he spent more time than ever as Country Neil, and had even less success.

Young's first album for Geffen was *Trans*, a curious mixture of throwaway pop and far-out electronica. When that bombed, Young returned to Nashville to record with Elliot Mazer and a band including Tim Drummond and Ben Keith. "It was like *Harvest* II," Young told *Rolling Stone*'s James Henke in 1988. "It was done in Nashville in only a few days, basically the same way *Harvest* was done." When they heard the tapes, however, Geffen told Young that the album was "too country" to be a hit, and refused to release it. "The technopop thing was happening, and they had Peter Gabriel, and they were totally into that kind of trip," said Young. "I guess they just saw me as some old hippy from the 60s still trying to make acoustic music." So much for the "commercial" *Harvest* sound.

Wilful as ever, and incensed by Geffen's ludicrous lawsuit, Neil Young released *Old Ways* in 1985. Derived partly from the sessions that Geffen had rejected and partly from new recordings, it is by far the most pure country album Young has ever made, much closer to mainstream country music than anything on *Harvest* or *Comes A Time*. Like all of Young's Geffen albums, it flopped. Perhaps they had been right to think that country music was no longer saleable; or perhaps, by that time, nothing short of a masterpiece could have rescued Young's career from the low to which it had sunk.

Miraculously, Young's career was eventually rescued by two successive masterpieces, neither of which sounded remotely like *Harvest*. His genre-hopping antics had left him facing the real risk of becoming an irrelevance, but Folkie Neil returned in angry style with 1989's *Freedom*. Reunited with Crazy Horse, he then proceeded to justify his "Godfather of Grunge" tag with some of the loudest rock 'n' roll ever made on 1990's *Ragged Glory*. By the time Country Neil made his next appearance, the music press was already eating out of his hand.

Harvest Moon wasn't recorded in Nashville and wasn't produced by Elliot Mazer, but the intent was obvious: this was an explicit sequel to *Harvest*, with The Stray Gators all present and correct. The reviews were ecstatic, the sales impressive. *Harvest Moon* was the concluding step on Young's road back to favour with critics and public alike.

Harvest Moon is perhaps a more consistent album than *Harvest* and, like the original, boasts melodies that any songwriter would kill to have produced. The tone is once again downbeat and sweetly melancholic, this time heavy with nostalgia, and The Stray Gators are as tasteful and restrained as ever. From the perspective of yet another decade, however, *Harvest Moon* also seems to share many of the failings of the original. There's clumsy political comment, this time about the environment; there are songs so slight they seem more thrown away than composed; there's even a Jack Nitzsche-arranged stinker in the tradition of 'There's A World'. It's full of pretty tunes and tasteful arrangements, but as before, superficial charm betrays a lack of emotional depth. Neil Young had made another very fine album, but once again, he had allowed craft to dominate art.

Harvest Track By Track

'Out On The Weekend'

Neil Young's first Nashville sessions may have been great fun for all concerned, but you wouldn't know that from the way *Harvest* begins. A ponderous, two-note bass line drags behind it a skeletal drum beat. Broken chords from Young's acoustic guitar drift by in the distance, to be joined there by a harmonica line best described as plaintive. The sparse arrangement builds slowly, before subsiding even further to make room for Young's unvarnished, warts-and-all voice: "Think I'll pack it in . . . "

The mood is one of resignation, perhaps even exhaustion. The song's narrator makes half-hearted plans to relocate, to "start a brand new day", but there's no conviction in his voice. Still haunted by the memory of a lost love, he can't hold on to his dreams of Los Angeles; his thoughts turn to her with a sad inevitability.

In 'Out On The Weekend', Neil Young wields few words with some skill. The verses, sung in the first person, are introspective, wistful; then, for the chorus, there's a sudden shift, the narrator standing outside himself. Rather than direct his pleading at the girl who's deserted him, he turns to the listener, begging us to

> *See the lonely boy*
> *Out on the weekend*
> *Trying to make it pay*

It's a surprising jump, and an effective one.

The song's use of detail is also striking. We never find out who the narrator's lost love is, or why she's gone, but we learn about the pictures on the wall and her big brass bed. This is a classic lyrical trick, particularly beloved of country songwriters; so often it's the small things that have the power to evoke a time, a place, or a person. It's all very well that "She's so fine / She's in my mind", but what makes the lonely boy's plight convincing are these tiny splinters of memory.

For all its wistful sadness, it seems likely that 'Out On The Weekend' is less autobiographical than many Neil Young songs. When *Harvest* was recorded, his relationship with Carrie Snodgress was at its height; it's hard to imagine that he seriously contemplated being the lonely boy, looking to make good on a Saturday night. Similarly, packing one's life up into a pickup truck and finding a bachelor pad in LA might be a romantic ideal, but Young had in fact just tied himself to a very large ranch in backwoods California. As for the pictures and the big brass bed, who knows?

'Out On The Weekend' exemplifies the finesse at the heart of the *Harvest* sound. It's the product of song-writing skill and craft rather than an outpouring of naked emotion, yet it's not indulgent. Young's years as a folk troubador and his ambitious work with Buffalo Springfield and Crosby, Stills & Nash had given him a grounding in the classical virtues of songwriting. He was sure-footed in his choice of melodies and harmonies and mature enough to keep them simple, ruthless in clearing away unnecessary lyrical clutter.

Nevertheless, 'Out On The Weekend' is still a relatively slight song, and could easily have been sunk by an unsympathetic treatment. What makes the version on *Harvest* special is the performance of Young and The Stray Gators. Buffalo Springfield or CSN might have allowed instrumental virtuosity or studio excess to suffocate such a delicate song, but here, Young projects a freshness and vulnerability that draws the listener in. Others would have recorded their vocals again and again, striving for perfection at the expense of expressiveness; Young laid the whole thing down live.

The immediacy of Young's approach to recording allows the song's virtues to shine through, but that's not to say that it doesn't benefit from The Stray Gators' musicianship. Young had evolved his minimalist approach to recording while making his earlier solo albums *Everybody Knows This Is Nowhere* and *After The Goldrush*. Those albums, though, had been recorded with raw, bar-band musicians, and bore the rough edges to prove it. 'Out On The Weekend' might have proved too fragile to survive the full garage-band onslaught.

This time, however, Young was working with musicians who were used to playing a song once and having it be note-perfect, and engineers who knew how to get it sounding good in a matter of minutes. The Stray Gators had both the disciplined musicianship that was lacking in Crazy Horse, and the self-effacing willingness to be sidemen that Crosby, Stills and Nash would never accept. The sessions for *Harvest* brought Young's garage-band aesthetic up against Nashville professionalism, and on 'Out On The Weekend', the combination worked perfectly.

'Harvest'

Neil Young's words are often straightforwardly autobiographical, but his back catalogue also contains its fair share of obscure lyrics. His first solo album goes sharply off the rails with the nine-minute allegorical ramble of 'Last Trip To Tulsa', while *After The Goldrush* opens with 'Tell Me Why', which is portentous but, as Young later admitted, meaningless. *Harvest* itself closes with the clumsy surrealism of 'Words', and his follow-up *Time Fades Away* boasts the bizarre 'Yonder Stands The Sinner', as well as its title track. These songs are recognisably of a type: full of wild imagery, apparently allegorical in intent, and often heavy-handed in execution, they pop up regularly on Young's early albums.

'Harvest' is equally hard to understand, but has little in common with these epics. There's nothing to suggest an allegorical aspect to the lyrics, which are devoid of kings and sinners, and free of trees to be chopped down, tall ships to be sailed through empty harbours, or arrangements to be made with oneself. There are no riddles, internal contradictions or dramatic shifts of time and place, yet 'Harvest' is still undeniably obscure. Most of its lines are descriptive, plain, almost understated, but together they have no obvious message or story to convey.

In his biography *Shakey*, Jimmy McDonough says that 'Harvest' was inspired by Carrie Snodgress's stories about her eccentric family, and especially by her mother's repeated threats to commit suicide. This insight certainly helps to make sense of lines like "Did I see you down in a young girl's town / With your mother in so much pain?" and "Did she wake you up to tell you that it was only a change of plan?", but there seems to be more to the lyric. 'Harvest' can also be seen as belonging to another recognisable group of Neil Young songs: confessionals from a guilty man, trying to justify himself to his spurned or abandoned women. Perhaps the best of these, and among the best of all Young songs, is 'I Believe In You' from *After The Goldrush*: "Now that you've made yourself love me," he cries, "do you think I can change it in a day?" The theme is explored in the same album's 'Birds' and on 'Running Dry' from *Everybody Knows This Is Nowhere*, and seems to lie somewhere near the heart of 'Harvest'. There's a girl brimming over with feelings for the narrator, but he can't return them. "Dream up, dream up," he sings, "let me fill your cup / With the promise of a man". The girl is too willing to give, and he can only harvest some.

Whatever 'Harvest' meant to its creator, it's much more lyrically affecting than his more extreme flights of fancy. The restrained language and everyday imagery provide much more for the listener to connect with than Young's grandiose meditations on time or space.

The understated style of the lyric is matched by the straightforward, wistful charm of the music. Young's songwriting craft, apparent on 'Out On The Weekend', is also very much in evidence here. Lacking any real distinction between verse and chorus, it may be simple, but it's hugely effective. In many ways, 'Harvest' is the closest thing the album has to a true country song, with its honky-tonk piano and mournful yet major-key feel.

Again, the recording sees the song pared down to the bare essentials, and all the more powerful for it. All the songs on *Harvest* were recorded live, and in most cases, a lot of work was needed at the mixing stage to recapture the feel of the sessions. Not so with the title track: what appears on the album is the live two-track mix, exactly as it was heard in Quadrafonic Studios that day. The performance is driven mainly by the piano. Neil Young is not exactly Alfred Brendel, but when a piano part is this central to one of his songs, it's usually him that plays it. Here, however, it's the turn of Nashville session musician John Harris to shine. At Young's insistence, meanwhile, Kenny Buttrey made his drumming even more minimal than on 'Out On The Weekend'; Buttrey played one-handed, using only the bass and snare drums.

'A Man Needs A Maid'

Listening to *Harvest* today, it's hard to believe that 'A Man Needs A Maid' provoked heated controversy on its release. In some quarters, it seems, the song was seriously understood as a statement of male chauvinism, a defence of the idea that every man really should have a female servant. Either the champions of sexism had failed to actually listen to the song, or their feminist opponents were painfully over-sensitive, for the obvious theme of 'A Man Needs A Maid' is not masculine power but the weakness of the male sex. It's less an expression of triumph over the female of the species than it is one of bewilderment and inadequacy.

'A Man Needs A Maid' is perhaps the most straight-forwardly confessional song on the album. Its opening verse, oddly omitted from the album's lyric sheet, expresses a blanket dismay at the many ways in which the narrator's life is changing. He no longer knows who to trust, he is haunted by "a shadow running through my days". These could be expressions of general angst, but they could also be references to the much-publicised conflicts within CSNY, and the heroin that would claim Danny Whitten's life.

Another verse offers some poetic autobiographical detail. "I was watching a movie with a friend," Young recounts, "I fell in love with the actress / She was playing a part that I could understand." Young's relationship with Carrie Snodgress had begun when he saw her in a film called *Diary Of A Mad Housewife*; so impressed was he by her performance that he'd sent her a note asking if they could meet.

Like 'Out On The Weekend', the song gains emotive force from an abrupt switch in the focus of the narration.

From the measured, descriptive language of the verses, Young unexpectedly turns to address the listener, asking repeatedly "When will I see you again?" Like the protagonist of 'Out On The Weekend' making his feeble plan to move to LA, he's been trying to convince himself that there's an easy solution to his problems, that a maid will provide female companionship without emotional involvement. Again, though, what comes through in the end is that only emotional attachment can solve these problems and chase away that shadow. "To live a love," he admits, "You've got to be 'part of '."

It's not clear what prompted Neil Young to record 'A Man Needs A Maid' with an orchestra. Live, Young performed it at the piano as a solo piece, sometimes segueing into 'Heart Of Gold'. For the BBC TV *Old Grey Whistle Test* recording, taped the week before the *Harvest* orchestral session, he produced a fine solo rendition, although by this time he had decided 'Heart Of Gold' sounded better on guitar.

Critics of the recorded version have complained that the song is too delicate to bear the full force of the London Symphony Orchestra. Jack Nitzsche's heavyweight arrangement has often been accused of turning a fragile ballad into a monument to pretension, and even those who love it must question whether it really belongs between two modest country-pop songs like 'Harvest' and 'Heart Of Gold'. "Some people thought the arrangement was overdone," admitted Young in the liner notes to his *Decade* compilation, "but Bob Dylan told me it was one of his favourites. I listened closer to Bob."

It would be fair to say that Nitzsche's work on 'A Man Needs A Maid' is not as sympathetic as his earlier arrangements for 'Expecting To Fly' or 'The Old Laughing Lady'. Here, his treatment forces grandeur onto a humble song, but it isn't without its own qualities. The one place where classical composers could still make money in the 60s was Hollywood, and Nitzsche had become an accomplished composer and arranger for the screen. On 'A Man Needs A Maid', he uses the orchestra to underline the dynamics of Young's performance in the same way a film composer might reinforce the twists and turns of some high melodrama. As Young pounds the piano and launches into his impassioned cry "A ma-ai-ai-aid", a solo piccolo posts a warning note, before swirling strings soar upwards. It's neither subtle nor sensitive, but in a world where violins are often used merely to add a touch of colour to a conventional rock arrangement, it stands out as a genuine attempt to turn a pop song into an orchestral piece.

'Heart Of Gold'

Neil Young's only major hit single, 'Heart Of Gold' reached No. 1 in Britain and America, and remains his best-known song. Even today, when you hear a Neil Young song on the radio, nine times out of ten it's this one. Its hit status was obvious to Elliot Mazer and Kenny Buttrey as soon as they heard the studio playback, and had a profound effect on the sales of the whole album.

'Heart Of Gold' is one of few Neil Young songs that sounds like it could have been someone else's. On hearing it, Bob Dylan accused Young of a conscious attempt to pastiche him, but there's little apart from some gauche harmonica playing to mark it out as especially Dylanesque. It's not that the song sounds like anyone else in particular; it just has the quality of a great pop song. Like the classics turned out by staff songwriters in the Brill Building or Tin Pan Alley, it doesn't give the impression of being written to make a point, or to lay bare the writer's own feelings. It's simply a good song written for the sake of writing a good song.

For all its ubiquity, 'Heart Of Gold' is a slight affair: an effortless, straightforward melody set to a sparse four-chord backing, with a lyric amounting to barely ten lines. Young is adept enough to avoid falling into rock 'n' roll cliché, but at the same time, there's little of the emotional directness that characterises his most powerful work. The only hint of autobiography is a glancing mention of Redwood, California, where Neil's ranch is located. Other than that, the theme is simply the search for love, couched in the most general terms.

Young's complaint that this song had placed him in the middle of the road is too harsh, but most fans would agree that his journey into the ditch was ultimately more rewarding.

If the song verges on the throwaway, so did the recording session: according to Elliot Mazer, the entire track was done in less than two hours, including James Taylor and Linda Ronstadt's vocal harmonies. The results demonstrate just how effective Young's live-and-direct approach can be. The Stray Gators provide the perfect reading: there's not an unnecessary note, and little touches like Ben Keith's descending steel-guitar run to follow the line "And I'm getting old" are beautifully apt. Listen closely and you'll hear that there are actually two acoustic guitars on the record: Neil Young cheerfully thrashes away in the right-hand speaker, while Nashville songwriter Teddy Irwin makes an uncredited appearance in the left, adding some deft harmonics and nice details. Meanwhile, Kenny Buttrey managed to unbend Young's minimalism sufficiently to play a neat hi-hat rhythm; Young and Elliot Mazer must have liked it, as the hi-hat is mixed louder than any of the other drums.

'Are You Ready For The Country?'

'Heart Of Gold' and the first two tracks on *Harvest* temper Neil Young's spontaneity with Nashville slick-

ness, to impressive effect. At the end of side one, however, we're treated to a glimpse of the rawness that
Young would bring to his later albums. A chaotic false
start, complete with insane giggling, gives way to a
shambling, piano-led stomp. Ben Keith's tasteful pedal
steel is barely audible; in its place, non-guitarist Jack
Nitzsche plays slide on a cheap electric guitar Young
had bought for him on a whim. The queasy tunelessness
of the result adds an unsettling edge to the performance.

The Stray Gators are present and correct, yet no
longer in the familiar confines of Quadrafonic Studios.
They're in a barn and they sound like it, but there's no
doubting the force with which they and Young tear into
the song. So far, so promising, but the question that
springs to mind is whether 'Are You Ready For The
Country?' is really worth tearing into. The melody is
as basic as that of 'Harvest' or 'Out On The Weekend',
but not as good, while the lyric is equally forgettable.
There doesn't seem to be a coherent point to the song
except to warn that "the country" is a sinister and dan-
gerous place. We have to go there, Young and the
listener, for some unexplained reason; but it's an experience we need to be ready for.

What "the country" is is not explained, but Neil
Young clearly doesn't mean Belgium. Although the
South isn't mentioned by name, 'Are You Ready For
The Country' seems to be of a piece with side two's

'Alabama' and its precursor, 'Southern Man' from *After The Goldrush*. Yet these songs are explicitly political, albeit heavy-handed: 'Are You Ready For The Country' has nothing to say about the civil rights struggle. Its perception of the South is less one of race hatred and prejudice than it is of vague, nameless, Gothic dread. It could be an interesting theme, but not when it's handled this clumsily. "I was talking to the preacher," Young explains, "said God was on my side / Then I ran into the hangman / He said 'It's time to die.' " If the reverend and the executioner are supposed to be allegorical figures, they're about the most clichéd examples Young could have chosen.

The question that is the song's title could also be seen as one of musical genre, as Peter Doggett pointed out when he appropriated it for his book about the country-rock phenomenon. Addressing his audience of hippies, folkies and rockers, Young seems to be saying "I'm going to make country music. Are you sure you're ready for this?"

For a few years after the release of Dylan's landmark *Nashville Skyline* in 1969, it seemed that everyone from the Stones to Sinatra was wheeling out their dobros and pedal steel guitars. Country music, or at least country-rock, was flavour of the month. Yet the same twenty-something hippies who would buy *Harvest* in droves had been used to thinking of the country music scene as evil incarnate. Whatever your cause, be it feminism, civil rights, pacifism, or good taste in clothes, country music had something to offend.

When Young had told a Carnegie Hall audience that he would be appearing on *The Johnny Cash Show* he'd been heckled: "Why? Why with Cash?" a voice had shouted, adding the word "man" as befitted a beatnik finishing a sentence. Despite Dylan's efforts, a large proportion of young Americans were still suspicious of, or downright hostile to, country music. Perhaps the heavy-handed lyrics to 'Alabama' and 'Are You Ready For The Country?' were an attempt on Young's part to tell his audience that it was still all right to like him. Even though he was appearing on *The Johnny Cash Show* and recording in Nashville, he seemed to be saying, he hadn't given up on good, liberal values.

On the strength of 'Are You Ready For The Country?', Neil Young wasn't about to turn into Faron Young in any case. Its ramshackle arrangement is closer to the blues than to country music, and few of the musical trademarks of that genre are present here or anywhere else on *Harvest*.

'Old Man'

When he recorded several of *Harvest*'s best songs in his session for the BBC, Young took it upon himself to explain 'Old Man' to his audience. The ranch he'd just bought was looked after by an elderly foreman called Louie Avilla, and the song was about him — or, more precisely, directed at him. "Old man, take a look at my life," Young implores, "I'm a lot like you." Is he trying to justify his and Carrie's decision to up sticks and move away from the city to the middle of nowhere? There is, after all, "so much more" to find; perhaps here are the "things that don't get lost", the people to whom he can roll home, the someone who will love him "the whole day through".

It's hard not to see other lines in 'Old Man' as directed elsewhere, however. In one of the best couplets in any Neil Young song, he insists that it "Doesn't mean that much to me / To mean that much to you." Perhaps the attraction of living in the country, with an old ranch-hand for company, was that Young no longer had to keep up appearances. In the light of Young's career, though, it sounds as much like a statement of his attitude to celebrity.

When he first tasted success as a member of Buffalo Springfield, Young reportedly found the experience an uneasy one, and later blamed his repeated departures from that band on the pressures of expectation and publicity. "My nerves couldn't handle the trip," he told Cameron Crowe. He'd moved out of LA proper to Topanga Canyon to "get out to the sticks for a while and relax," but had eventually left "because I couldn't handle all the people who kept coming up all the time." And that was before *After The Goldrush* and CSNY had made him a real superstar. To top it all, he was worried that crowds might be a trigger for his occasional epileptic seizures.

Neil Young's commercial success had also come at the expense of some hostility from the critics. Although reaction to *After The Goldrush* had been mostly positive, it had suffered a stinging review in *Rolling Stone*, while CSNY's best-selling *Déjà Vu* album had been greeted with a sense of disappointment. His back injury had forced Young into a long period of inactivity, to dwell on such things. "I spent two years flat on my back," he told Crowe. "I had a lot of time to think about what had happened to me." On the ranch, Young's every word wouldn't be scrutinised for its political significance; he wouldn't be accused of selling out, pestered by hangers-on, or nagged about when CSNY would record again. And 'Old Man' could serve as a warning notice to any critic who chose to pan *Harvest*.

In purely musical terms, 'Old Man' is perhaps the absolute high-water point of Neil Young's craft as a songwriter. Few of his other songs can boast such a lovely guitar part, a delicate piece of minor-key finger-picking that owes more to folk music than country or pop. As on 'Out On The Weekend' and 'Harvest', he uses broken and extended chords, in a sequence that is both more complex and more subtle than those usually found in Young songs. There's a memorable melody, wistful in the verses and impassioned in the chorus. On the recording, The Stray Gators' usual impeccable tastefulness is augmented by Andy McMahon's piano playing and nicely undercut by James Taylor's spiky six-string banjo. Like 'Heart Of Gold', it steers a perfect course between spontaneity and slickness. Unsurprisingly, 'Old Man' was chosen as the second single from the album, although it failed to match the achievements of the first.

'There's A World'

'There's A World' is the second of two orchestral numbers on *Harvest*. Critics of 'A Man Needs A Maid' maintain that that song isn't well suited to the orchestral arrangement, but most agree that it stands up on its own. In the case of 'There's A World', however, it's tempting to say that the orchestral arrangement is the only element with any merit. Again, Jack Nitzsche deploys his film-composing chops with considerable flair, incorporating daring touches like the impossibly long pedal note the strings are asked to hold throughout the last verse. Billy Walker, reviewing *Harvest* in *Sounds*, described the results as sounding "a little like the theme from Ben Hur".

Nevertheless, all the thundering timps and sawing strings can't disguise the fact that 'There's A World' is one of the worst songs Neil Young has ever written. Every artist who stays the course for 30 years is bound to have a few lapses, and Young is no exception. Yet there's usually an interesting idea at the core of even his most embarrassing efforts: if they don't work, it's because the idea was developed clumsily, or because too much was built on a slight metaphor, or occasionally because the concept was barking mad in the first place. In 'Will To Love' from *American Stars & Bars*, for instance, Young develops into a bizarrely awful seven-minute epic the whimsical image of himself as a leaping salmon. At a scant three minutes, 'There's A World' is arguably more listenable than 'Will To Love', but its fault is less excusable. It is, to be blunt, dull. If there is an idea at the heart of 'There's A World', it seems to be little more than a crass reworking of the 'All the world's a stage' speech from *As You Like It*. The melody is insipid, the lyrics platitudinous and clichéd. Young's best work is almost uncomfortable in its emotional honesty, but this shows nothing of the man or his talent.

'Alabama'

The rock song is about as bad a vehicle for political comment as you can get. The idea that it might be possible to say anything worthwhile about class struggle or the situation in the Middle East in three verses and a chorus, whilst getting it all to rhyme and fitting it to a catchy tune, is fundamentally daft. To compound the problem, most rock stars are pretty inept commentators on politics; but it doesn't stop them trying.

Neil Young's interest in politics could be called sporadic. *Harvest* marks the tail end of his first, and least interesting, period of political comment, during which Young produced a number of songs based around the standard themes of the alternative movement. 'Ohio', a hit for CSNY, was a shocked response to the shooting of four student protesters at Kent State University; 'War Song', Young's duet with Graham Nash, comments on the shooting of Alabama's Governor George Wallace. The title track of *After The Goldrush* marks Young's adherence to the green movement, while 'Alabama' follows that album's 'Southern Man' in addressing civil rights and the perceived backwardness of the American South. Both 'Ohio' and 'Alabama', incidentally, take up places in a minor tradition of Neil Young songs named after bits of America, along with the likes of 'LA',

'Hawaii', 'Kansas', 'Florida', 'Albuquerque' and 'Philadelphia'.

For the rest of the 70s, Young abstained from political comment. The turn of the decade saw him apparently reborn as a right-winger, voicing support for protectionism, praise for Ronald Reagan's tough-guy foreign policy and dismay at the hardships then afflicting farming families. His affection for country music seemed then to be matched by a down-home, family-values political outlook, not so far removed from that of the rednecks he'd roasted in songs like 'Alabama'.

As the 80s drew to a close, Young's views appeared to shift again. He regained critical acceptance with 1989's *Freedom* and its caustic "what has the world come to?" songs such as 'Rockin' In The Free World' and 'Crime In The City', before expressing outspoken opposition to the 1991 Gulf War. *Harvest Moon*, released in 1992, boasts the anti-war 'War Of Man' and the ecological diatribe 'Natural Beauty'. Since then, Young has tended to keep his silence on political issues.

Young's left-leaning songs have usually found more favour with the critics than his odes to conservatism, but 'Alabama' has received a rough ride over the years. It has been called clumsy, heavy-handed and simplistic; but the most persistent criticism directed at 'Alabama' is that it is, in the words of *Rolling Stone*'s Jim Miller, "an unblushing rehash of 'Southern Man'." 'Alabama' is, as many rock critics will tell you, redundant, because Young had already tackled the same subject in an earlier song.

'Alabama' does occupy similar lyrical territory to 'Southern Man', but this hardly justifies writing it off altogether. Where is it written that songwriters may not address the same subject more than once? Bacharach and David never came under fire for writing too many songs about heartbreak, while Chubby Checker twisted and twisted again until he must have been dizzy. Why, then, should Young be castigated for addressing the same theme in two songs?

The claim that the lyrics to 'Alabama' are inherently objectionable has more substance to it. There is something patronising in the way Young addresses an entire American state as if it were a wayward child. When he sings "You got the rest of the Union to help you along / What's going wrong?" you half expect him to add "You're letting me down, you're letting the school down and most of all you're letting yourself down." The image of the Southern states presented here depends as much on caricature and hearsay as it does on thoughtful observation. In short, 'Alabama' suffers from the same shortcomings that afflict so many political rock songs. In these respects, it's no worse than most, and a lot less bad than some. There are certainly many more crass political songs in Young's own back catalogue, from 'War Song' to 'Mideast Vacation'.

Interestingly, in the interview that accompanies the DVD-A release of *Harvest*, Neil Young suggests that the driving force behind 'Alabama' may have been personal rather than political. "I just put the name of a state in the South on it, because it fit the image of what I was trying to say. Actually the song is more about a personal thing than it is about a state, you know, and I'm just using that name and that state to hide whatever it is that I have to hide." In the same breath, however, Young goes on to admit "I don't know what that means," and it is difficult to see how he could have written 'Alabama' without any political intent. It's conceivable that he saw the plight of the Southern state as some kind of metaphor for his own state of mind, but the idea of Young's psyche being filled with banjos or old folks in white robes seems forced at best. More likely, perhaps, is that when the interview was filmed, during the final sessions on Young's ranch, he was already anticipating the critical response to 'Alabama', and sought to play down its political intent. On watching the interview it's also easy to believe that he was simply stoned and saying the first thing that came to mind.

Whatever provoked Neil Young to write 'Alabama', to focus on its shortcomings is to ignore the song's many strengths. The lyric may not be the most profound piece of political commentary in the world, but it boasts some powerful imagery: Cadillacs in the ditch, banjos playing through the broken glass, and so on. The music is even better. Elsewhere on *Harvest*, The Stray Gators demonstrate that they can be subtle, reflective, restrained, tasteful. On 'Alabama', they reveal their muscle.

As an electric guitarist Neil Young is best known for playing a 1953 Gibson Les Paul nicknamed Old Black, but like any self-respecting rock star he has a collection of 50 or so other instruments. Many of these have found their way onto his records, especially in the early 70s when Old Black went missing. For the barn sessions on *Harvest*, he turned to a hollow-bodied Gretsch White Falcon guitar he'd traded from Stephen Stills the previous year.

The White Falcon was, for quite a while, the most expensive production guitar in the world, although Gretsch instruments have never been as widely coveted as Gibsons or Fenders. The White Falcon's appearance verged on the kitsch, and it confused simple-minded guitarists by providing more controls than a small nuclear reactor. The particular version Young played on 'Alabama' and 'Words' was especially complicated, being one of very few electric guitars designed to be used in stereo. Split pickups allowed the guitarist to take the sound from the treble strings and the bass strings out independently to two different guitar amplifiers, in Young's case a pair of Fender Customs. The result is a guitar sound that seems to spread out across the entire stereo field, with low notes in the left speaker and high notes in the right.

The White Falcon's split pickup might have been just a gimmick from the early days of stereo, but the way Neil Young uses it on 'Alabama' is remarkable. His muted picking brings stabbing notes first from one speaker, then the other, as though we were hearing not one but two guitarists, playing with an unnatural empathy. The electric guitar has seldom sounded so menacing, and Young's growling rhythm and piercing lead notes are tracked perfectly by Kenny Buttrey's bare-bones drumming. The build to the chorus is beautifully judged, and when Young and his celebrity backing singers let rip, there's an almost physical sense of release.

'The Needle And The Damage Done'

Wander into a folk club or student bedsit, and you'd be forgiven for thinking that every acoustic guitar sold came with instructions as to how to play 'The Needle And The Damage Done'. That descending picking pattern still provides a challenge to aspiring musicians, but the song's impact has faded with the years.

'The Needle And The Damage Done' was Young's first overt anti-heroin statement, and was inspired by the sorry state to which the drug had brought Danny Whitten of Crazy Horse. When Young had first encountered The Rockets, as they were originally called, Whitten had been their *de facto* leader, a fine guitarist and singer. He remained central when they became Young's backing band, singing harmonies and providing inspired foil for Young's unhinged guitar solos. Crazy Horse with Danny Whitten backed Young on only one complete album, his second. *Everybody Knows This Is Nowhere* was a perfect contrast to the self-effacing polish of his first: in its fresh, bloody and breezy roughness, Young had finally found what he considered the perfect mode of self-expression.

Young's third solo album was intended to be a repeat performance. By the time Young set up a studio in his Topanga Canyon basement to record it, however, Danny Whitten had become a junkie. His performances on tour in 1970 had been increasingly shambolic, and Young eventually decided that it would be impossible to work with Crazy Horse while Whitten was still on smack. *After The Goldrush*, which would be Young's breakthrough album as a solo artist, was consequently recorded with a motley amalgamation of collaborators from other Young projects.

Danny Whitten was a close friend, and gelled with Young musically as few others could. Dropping him was a painful move for Young, and his attempts to repair the damage eventually ended in disaster. When he put together a band to take *Harvest* on the road, he saw it as an opportunity to rehabilitate Whitten. Whitten came to the ranch to rehearse for the *Time Fades Away* tour, but he was too far gone to play even the simplest tune. Sent home by a despairing Young, he overdosed and died the same night.

Whitten's death, and the later overdose of CSNY roadie Bruce Berry, have fed into some of Young's greatest music. *Tonight's The Night*, perhaps his most acclaimed album, is a truly spine-chilling farewell to his lost friends. 'The Needle And The Damage Done', however, was written sometime on that 1970 tour with Crazy Horse, while Whitten's addiction was apparent but before it led to tragedy. It makes Young's dislike of the drug obvious enough, but it doesn't pack the emotive punch that *Tonight's The Night* does.

As with 'Alabama', there's a curious whiff of condescension about the lyrics. On *Tonight's The Night*, Neil Young would become a songwriter torn apart by grief and guilt, desperately searching for catharsis and an end to pain. Here, he's the wise schoolmaster or thoughtful judge, dishing out difficult truths in a pained "hurts me more than it hurts you" fashion. Young seems to say that heroin addiction turns you into a pain in the ass, into the kind of person who's constantly knocking at one's cellar door and demanding "more". As a consequence, it's Young's sad duty, because he "love[s] the man", to say "enough" — or at least to write a song about how bad heroin is.

Of course, heroin does turn good people into pains in the ass, and Young was ahead of his peers in picking up on the dark side of drug culture as early as 1970. One can but imagine the frustration, anger and sadness that Whitten's addiction must have brought Young, but 'The Needle And The Damage Done' only hints at an expression of these feelings.

Neil Young's own analysis of *Harvest* — "It was probably the finest record I ever made, but that's really a restricting adjective for me" — is borne out most clearly by 'The Needle And The Damage Done'. It's this song, above all, that demonstrates how Young's art is restricted by finesse. That guitar part is intricate and satisfying to play, but demands control from the player rather than abandonment. The lyrics are precious, weighed down by smart-ass contradictions like "I caught you knocking at my cellar door" and "Milk-blood to keep from running out". The live performance is a model of restraint, Young's pitching unusually spot-on, his fretwork and rhythm flawless. Yet Neil Young at his best is a great performer precisely because he can ignore such musical niceties to nail the feeling at the core of a song.

'The Needle And The Damage Done' is a pleasant song, but a Neil Young song about the devastation wrought by heroin shouldn't be pleasant. It should be like 'Tonight's The Night': angry, bitter, hurt, confused, twisted, shocked and cathartic. The destruction wrought by heroin would go on to inspire some of Young's most heartfelt music: here, though, his head rules his heart.

'Words (Between The Lines Of Age)'

The polite applause of Californian students is rudely cut off by *Harvest*'s final track. Distorted guitar and pounding drums hint at the presence of the same power behind 'Alabama', but the song never gathers enough pace to rock. Instead, it settles into a despondent, intensely weary chug, with Young alternately declaiming incomprehensible lyrics and spitting out pinched fragments of guitar solo. There's none of the anger that drives 'Alabama' or 'Southern Man'; gone too is the sense of joy and freedom that characterised Young's rocking out on *Everybody Knows This Is Nowhere*. 'Words (Between The Lines Of Age)' is both baffling and baffled, an oblique reaction to the confusing ways of the world.

The 70s were the heyday of unusual time signatures. From Jethro Tull to Pink Floyd, no self-respecting progressive rock band could miss the chance to riff in 7/8 or 5/4 every now and again. However, Neil Young is no Robert Fripp, and 'Words' is, as far as I know, unique among his solo output in its experiments with musical meter. The opening riff and instrumental sections alternate bars of 6/8 and 5/8 time, while the verse and chorus revert to conventional 4/4. The results only add to the song's feeling of alienation; allied to Young's refusal to ever launch into a lengthy, melodic guitar solo, they give 'Words' an unsettled, choppy tension, never allowing it to relax into a smooth groove.

The lyrics are among Young's most opaque. Laden with symbolic characters and gestures, they suggest a puzzle or riddle, but no key is provided. Who are "someone and someone"? Why would they want to plant pondweed in their lawn? Why should the king start laughing and talking in rhyme? The feeling of bewilderment is reinforced by the way the lyrics jump, apparently at random, between present and past tenses. It's debatable whether Young ever intended it to be made complete sense of, yet it still seems to carry a lot of significance for him. Other exercises in cryptic wordplay, such as 'Harvest' and 'Tell Me Why', have been absent from Young's set lists for years, but he still plays 'Words' 30 years on.

'Words (Between The Lines Of Age)' is perhaps best understood as another song about the perils of stardom, which appear to have been prominent in Young's mind throughout his early career. It seems like an attempt to convey the confusion that comes of trying to live a normal life when one's face is familiar to millions. Suddenly, everyone feels that they know him: out on the road, they're bringing him presents and saying hello. People appear friendly, but at the same time they're nosing around in his pond. The superstar Neil Young is public property; his mind belongs to his audience, but he imagines himself as reversing the situation, as a junkman who dreams of owning other people's thoughts. Young may be the king, and his ranch a castle, but what kind of life is it that is lived "a bit at a time"?

The Personnel

By the time he started putting together *Harvest* in 1971, Neil Young was already one of the biggest acts on Warner Bros' books. His star status is demonstrated by the roll-call of famous names who became involved in recording the album. Not only could he call upon stars like James Taylor and Linda Ronstadt to provide backing vocals: on *Harvest* he used some of Nashville's best-regarded session musicians, not to mention one of London's most prestigious orchestras, while the engineers and producers who worked on the album were at the top of their professions.

ELLIOT MAZER was something of an unusual figure in the Nashville music scene. He'd entered the music business in the early 60s as an A & R man and producer for Prestige Records in New York, and soon built up an impressive list of production credits in pop and jazz music. Unusually, he was also given the opportunity to see how the studio business worked in Tennessee: "I was taken to Nashville in 1963 to work on an album with El Trio Los Panchos, a famous Mexican group. I helped them cut an album of Hank Williams songs in Spanish and I got them to cut a Spanish version of the Beatles song 'Girl': 'Muchacha'. The trio sang and played their guitars, the Nashville 'A' team of Grady Martin, Harold Bradley, Buddy Harmon, Hargus 'Pig' Robbins and The Jordanaires doing the 'Ahhgirrrl-aaahh's. It was a great single and probably my biggest selling 45. The studio was the original Quanset Hut that Owen Bradley had built and used for many great records."

Prior to working with Neil Young on *Harvest*, he'd produced several important albums. One such was *Cheap Thrills* by Big Brother & The Holding Company, the record that brought Janis Joplin to the ears of the world. Another was Linda Ronstadt's *Silk Purse*, but perhaps the most significant in terms of its connections with *Harvest* were the two albums by Area Code 615. A "supergroup" of session musicians including Stray Gators drummer Kenny Buttrey and imaginatively named after the Nashville telephone code, their experiments in combining country and R & B had been taped by Mazer at bassist Wayne Moss's garage-cum-studio, Cinderella Sound. The influence of these two records far outweighed their sales, which were limited by the band's inability to tour due to session commitments.

Having produced Neil Young's next album of new material after *Harvest*, the ill-fated *Time Fades Away*, Mazer has gone on to work with Young on many other occasions, usually when Country Neil is in evidence. Among Elliot Mazer's Neil Young productions are the unreleased *Homegrown* album, which Young shelved in favour of *Tonight's The Night*, and the country album Geffen rejected in 1983. Most recently, he's been responsible for remixing *Harvest* in 5.1 surround for the high-resolution DVD-Audio release.

GLYN JOHNS is one of the most celebrated British recording engineers and producers, and was already in hot demand by the time he recorded the London Symphony Orchestra for *Harvest*. In 1971 he had produced The Who's *Who's Next* and The Faces' *A Nod's As Good As A Wink . . .*, and engineered The Stones' *Sticky Fingers*. He would soon go on to produce The Stones' *Exile On Main Street* and The Eagles' first two albums *On The Border* and *Desperado*.

BERNARD 'JACK' NITZSCHE enjoyed perhaps the longest and most complex relationship with Neil Young of any collaborator. He'd been involved in the Hollywood music business for a decade by the time he met Young, starting out as a music copyist before becoming a song-writer, composer and arranger. He collaborated with Sonny Bono and Lee Hazlewood, and was Phil Spector's arranger of choice for several years, providing character-istic orchestral settings for his ambitious production efforts like The Ronettes' 'Be My Baby'. Later, he worked with The Rolling Stones and wrote or co-wrote a number of successful songs including 'Needles And Pins', a hit for The Searchers in 1964. In the 70s he would become a successful composer of film soundtracks including *The Exorcist* and *One Flew Over The Cuckoo's Nest*.

Neil Young and Jack Nitzsche first worked together in 1967, when Young's band Buffalo Springfield went into the studio to record their second album. Young had written an ambitious multi-part epic called 'Ex-pecting To Fly', and called upon Nitzsche to provide an orchestral arrangement. The pair became close friends, and when Young secured a solo record contract follow-ing the demise of the Springfield, he was quick to call on Nitzsche. The latter's influence is obvious on the resulting album: side two opens with an instrumental Nitzsche composition on which Young doesn't appear at all, while Young originals are treated to complex, multi-layered arrangements. "It took me and Jack Nitzsche a month to put down the tracks for 'The Old Laughing Lady'," Young later claimed.

Although Young soon turned his back on the elaborate production techniques employed on his debut album, he continued to work with Jack Nitzsche. Their relationship was not always comfortable: both were intense and sometimes mulish personalities, and Nitzsche was reputedly a heavy drinker with something of a temper. Nevertheless, it's clear that Young valued Nitzsche as a powerful creative force, and involved him in his projects even when he had no plans to add elaborate orchestral arrangements. As well as arranging and producing the two orchestral numbers on *Harvest*, Nitzsche was also present at the sessions on Young's ranch; although he wasn't a guitarist, Young persuaded him to play slide on 'Are You Ready For The Country?' Following the release of *Harvest*, Young and The Stray Gators set out on the ill-fated *Time Fades Away* tour with Nitzsche on piano. Young and Nitzsche continued to work together on and off, and *Harvest Moon* included an orchestral ballad that was squarely in the tradition of 'A Man Needs A Maid'. The partnership was eventually broken by Nitzsche's death in 2000.

HENRY LEWY is another big name in the world of engineering and record production. Born in Germany, he arrived in America in 1940 as a refugee from the Nazi regime, and worked as a radio announcer before retraining as a recording engineer. From 1967 onwards he was staff engineer at Herb Alpert's A&M Studios, and has taken the controls on innumerable hit records, including most of Joni Mitchell's ambitious and critically acclaimed 70s output. By 1971 Lewy had already proved central to the birth of the country-rock movement, having produced The Flying Burrito Brothers' landmark *Gilded Palace Of Sin* and *Burrito Deluxe* LPs. Perversely, 'The Needle And The Damage Done', his sole contribution to any Neil Young album, is the only song on *Harvest* to betray no country influence whatsoever.

KENNY BUTTREY "was the kind of drummer that ate engineers alive if they did not get a good drum sound and a good earphone mix," according to Elliot Mazer. His blunt attitude did not stop him becoming one of Nashville's first-call session musicians in the 60s; and unlike some, he was easily able to make the move into rock and country-rock. When Neil Young hired him to play on *Harvest*, Buttrey was already well known outside the Nashville circuit, not only for his work on Bob Dylan's *Blonde On Blonde* and *Nashville Skyline* albums, but for the two albums he made with Area Code 615. After jumping ship during the acrimonious *Time Fades Away* tour, Buttrey returned to his career as a session player, and amassed one of the most impressive list of credits possible. Eventually, like the rest of The

Stray Gators, he returned to back Neil Young on *Harvest Moon*.

TIM DRUMMOND also had an impressive musical pedigree before becoming a Stray Gator. His introduction to the big time came as a touring musician with Conway Twitty in the latter's early days as a rockabilly star; he'd also been the only white man in James Brown's Famous Flames. The pace of Brown's tour schedule eventually wore him out, and he settled in Nashville as a session player. After recording *Harvest* and joining Young on the *Time Fades Away* tour he relocated to LA, where he has backed innumerable big names including Bob Dylan, The Beach Boys, JJ Cale and Ry Cooder. He's been one of a roster of two or three bass players that Neil Young has used on most of his albums: Drummond's include *On The Beach*, *Unplugged* and, of course, *Harvest Moon*.

BEN KEITH was a last-minute addition to the *Harvest* band. Arriving halfway through the session, he didn't even realise that Neil Young was a solo artist as well as a member of CSNY. "We cut half the album before he even introduced himself," he later said. Since then he's been one of Young's most constant musical collaborators: it would be far quicker to list the Young albums he hasn't appeared on than the ones he has. Of all The Stray Gators, he was the most deeply rooted in country music, and had long been known in Nashville for his work with Patsy Cline. His appearance on *Harvest* was largely responsible for bringing him to the attention of the musical world outside that city, and he went on to work with The Band, Linda Ronstadt, JJ Cale and many others. He's also found success as a producer, most notably with Jewel's debut album *Pieces Of You*, which sold over five million copies.

JAMES TAYLOR was in much the same position as Neil Young when they went to Nashville to appear on *The Johnny Cash Show*. His 1970 multi-platinum album *Sweet Baby James* had made him the most prominent of the new breed of sensitive, mellow singer-songwriters. *After The Goldrush* and *Harvest* saw Young placed firmly into the same pigeonhole, and the two had more in common. Young had a history of epilepsy, and had seen heroin claim one of his best friends; Taylor was a former addict who'd been hospitalised for mental illness. Whereas Young would soon overturn his categorisation as a sensitive singer-songwriter, however, Taylor remained more stylistically consistent, and had a string of hit albums throughout the 70s. *Harvest* and its sequel *Harvest Moon* remain the only Neil Young records he's appeared on.

LINDA RONSTADT was one of the first successful artists to combine country music with rock and folk. By the time she travelled to Nashville to join Young and Taylor on *The Johnny Cash Show*, she had already released two pioneering country-rock albums, while her third solo album, released in 1971, saw her backed by a band who would become The Eagles. The genre brought her success for most of the 70s, and she was astute enough to change musical tack when punk and new wave hit. As well as appearing on a number of Neil Young albums, including *Homegrown*, *Freedom*, *Harvest Moon* and the more recent *Silver & Gold*, she has also recorded her own versions of several Young songs including 'Birds', 'I Believe In You' and her hit single 'Love Is A Rose', which she and Young had originally recorded for *Homegrown*.

DAVID CROSBY was a founder member of The Byrds, and the motive force behind some of their most daring musical experiments. Increasing tension within the band saw him forced out in 1967, and after producing Joni Mitchell's debut album he teamed up with Stephen Stills and Graham Nash to form CSN. Sessions for their first album went smoothly, but tensions mounted following its success and Young's addition to the band. Crosby's legendary drug habit contributed to the band's squabbles, and would eventually lead to prison and a liver transplant. He and Nash joined Young for the later stages of the *Time Fades Away* tour, and the four have worked together intermittently since, but it was not until 1988 that the second CSNY album proper, *American Dream*, was released.

GRAHAM NASH was an unlikely convert to the West Coast scene of the late 60s. He'd become a star as harmony singer and songwriter with clean-cut English pop band The Hollies, but had become frustrated by the failure of their 1967 psychedelic album *Butterfly*. The other Hollies wanted to keep their fan base happy by returning to mainstream pop; Nash left, moved to California and hooked up with Crosby and Stills. He's since released a number of albums as a solo artist and in various permutations of CSN: he and Crosby have been particularly close collaborators, recording a number of albums as a duo. Nash and Young released one single as a twosome, 1972's 'War Song'.

STEPHEN STILLS came to the West Coast from Texas via New York City. His first significant band was The Au Go Go Singers, who featured future Buffalo Springfield bassist Richie Furay; their 1965 tour of Canada would introduce Stills to Neil Young. From the very beginning, Buffalo Springfield revolved around the rivalry between Stills and Young, which was played out live in noisy guitar duels. It was Stills who would deliver the band's only hit, in the shape of 'For What It's Worth', and after their demise, he was soon back in the public eye with Crosby and Nash. Stills was a perfectionist in the studio, dominating the recording of their first album; when CSN became CSNY, the Young-Stills tension soon reasserted itself.

Stephen Stills began the 70s with a string of successful solo albums, while later CSN outings have also sold well. Although their relationship has often been stormy, Young and Stills have also found it creatively inspiring, and their 1976 LP *Long May You Run* is the only truly collaborative album Young has made apart from fullblown CSNY efforts.

Harvest On CD And DVD-Audio

Neil Young has become well known for his views on compact discs: he hates them. Some have painted him as a Luddite, but his opinion is not just blind prejudice against digital audio, and it's one he shares with *Harvest*'s producer Elliot Mazer. To be more precise, what Young and Mazer dislike is the particular digital format used for compact discs. Both feel that the 44.1 kHz sampling rate and 16-bit dynamic range are not up to the job of reproducing music and making it sound good.

It wasn't always thus. Young was actually one of the first rock stars to experiment with digital recording and synthesis, while Mazer had even helped to develop the technology with John Chowning's CCRMA team at Stanford University. Luckily for Warner Bros, the label managed to get *Harvest* released on CD before its creator went sour on the format. "I did the first CD remaster of the album and it sounded as good as it could back in the early 80s," says Elliot Mazer. "We thought early PCM [the system used for encoding sound digitally on CDs] sounded cool. Then one day we compared Springsteen's *Born To Run* CD against vinyl and were aghast at how much better the vinyl sounded."

Following that revelation and an unhappy experience with digital recording on his 1983 album *Everybody's Rocking*, Neil Young has been unwavering in his hostility to the compact disc. He's gone to the extreme of blocking the release of six of his albums on CD, including *Journey Through The Past*, *Time Fades Away* and *On The Beach*, and he releases all his new albums in the little-used HDCD format, which is compatible with ordinary CD players but offers better sound quality on special players.

For an early CD, *Harvest* is perfectly acceptable, although it arguably sounds a little sterile and cold compared to the vinyl version. It could certainly have been a lot worse: many classic albums were rendered almost unlistenable on their first CD release by incompetent analogue-to-digital transfers.

In 2003, however, the music industry is keen to do away with compact disc and replace it with one of two new high-resolution digital formats: DVD-Audio and Super Audio CD. At the time of writing, Warner Bros, Young's record label for most of his career, are committed to DVD-A, while the other three major music groups have opted for SACD. It seems unlikely that both formats will survive; and while audiophiles engage in heated debate about which sounds better, many hi-fi companies are making combo players that recognise both. Super Audio CDs are also compatible with old-fashioned, traditional CD players, although the improved sound quality is available only on an SACD player.

Keen to establish their chosen format, Warner Bros have been steadily reissuing classic catalogue material on DVD-A, often with extra material and always with a surround mix. Whether you believe that surround sound for music listening is a gimmick or a quantum leap forward, their policy of having the original producer oversee the surround mix where possible is laudable. The *Harvest* DVD-A was remixed into surround at Neil Young's Redwood Digital studio by Young and Elliot Mazer. They have not been as generous with the extras as some: it would have been nice to hear out-takes like the quiet version of 'Alabama' and the unreleased 'Bad Fog Of Loneliness', but the track listing remains unaltered. Bonus material does include an amusing, incoherent filmed interview with Young, a brief snippet of Mazer "behind the barn" and some of Joel Bernstein's photos from the barn sessions.

Both Young and Mazer are thoroughly converted to the sonic merits of DVD-A, which offers 24-bit recording at sample rates of up to 192 kHz, to the extent that Young is said to be happy to release his "missing six" albums in the format. However, it should be pointed out that buying the *Harvest* DVD-A doesn't automatically give you access to the audiophile Advanced Resolution version, despite the prominent assertion that "This disc plays on all DVD players." There are, in fact, no fewer than five different versions of the entire album on the disc. The conventional stereo mix is included twice, once as 192 kHz / 24-bit Advanced Resolution audio, and once in the rather less impressive Dolby Digital 2.0 format. The 5.1 surround mix appears three times, as 96 kHz / 24-bit Advanced Resolution audio and in both Dolby Digital 5.1 and DTS 5.1.

Despite the widespread acceptance of DVD as a video format, the vast majority of players don't support the high-resolution DVD-A standard: only listeners with DVD-A compatible players can listen to the Advanced Resolution audio either in stereo or surround. Anyone using an ordinary DVD player, and most people listening on computers with a DVD-ROM drive, will be able to hear only the Dolby or DTS versions. Since both formats use "lossy" data compression in order to fit all the information into a limited space, the sound quality is inevitably compromised: ironically, all Young's efforts to present his music in the best resolution possible will see many people listening in a format that's arguably less good than CD. In the case of *Harvest*, at least, the benefits of a new transfer from the original master tapes are obvious even on the DTS and Dolby versions.